PERSONAL FINANCE

in Plain English

**DEFINITIONS.
EXAMPLES.
USES.**

Michele Cagan, CPA
Bestselling Author of *Investing 101*

Adams Media
New York Amsterdam/Antwerp London Toronto Sydney New Delhi

Adams Media
An Imprint of Simon & Schuster, LLC
100 Technology Center Drive
Stoughton, Massachusetts 02072

First Adams Media hardcover edition
March 2025

ADAMS MEDIA and colophon
are registered trademarks of
Simon & Schuster, LLC.

For information about special discounts
for bulk purchases, please contact Simon &
Schuster Special Sales at 1-866-506-1949 or
business@simonandschuster.com.

The Simon & Schuster Speakers Bureau
can bring authors to your live event. For
more information or to book an event,
contact the Simon & Schuster Speakers
Bureau at 1-866-248-3049 or visit our
website at www.simonspeakers.com.

Interior design by Colleen Cunningham
Interior images © Adobe Stock/Yuriy,
Vector VA, pixelalex, Big Dream

Manufactured in the United States of
America

1 2025

Library of Congress Cataloging-in-
Publication Data
Names: Cagan, Michele, author.
Title: Personal finance in plain English /
Michele Cagan, CPA, bestselling author of
Investing 101.
Description: First Adams Media hardcover
edition. | Stoughton, Massachusetts: Adams
Media, 2025. | Series: Financial literacy
guide series | Includes index.
Identifiers: LCCN 2024045354 | ISBN
9781507223611 (hc) | ISBN 9781507223628
(ebook)
Subjects: LCSH: Finance, Personal.
Classification: LCC HG179 .C285 2025 |
DDC 332.024--dc23/eng/20241119
LC record available at https://lccn.loc
.gov/2024045354

ISBN 978-1-5072-2361-1
ISBN 978-1-5072-2362-8 (ebook)

Contents

Introduction 5

CHAPTER 1
Common Banking and Financial Services Terms 7

CHAPTER 2
Income and Net Worth 20

CHAPTER 3
Budgeting and Financial Planning 32

CHAPTER 4
Taxes 45

CHAPTER 5
Savings 56

CHAPTER 6
Insurance 64

CHAPTER 7
Borrowing Money and Establishing Credit 78

CHAPTER 8
Credit Cards 91

CHAPTER 9
Unsecured Loans: Student Loans and Personal Loans 100

CHAPTER 10
Mortgages, Home Loans, and Auto Loans 113

CHAPTER 11
Dealing with Debt 127

CHAPTER 12
Investing Terms 139

CHAPTER 13
Stocks and Bonds 150

CHAPTER 14
**Mutual Funds, Exchange-Traded Funds (ETFs),
and Real Estate Investment Trusts (REITs)** 162

CHAPTER 15
Currency, Crypto, and Non-Fungible Tokens (NFTs) 174

CHAPTER 16
Retirement Planning 186

CHAPTER 17
Estate Planning 196

Index 205

Introduction

Navigating all the pieces of your financial life can be hard—and confusing. To succeed, you need to both understand and use the economic terms that define and direct your personal finances. For example, you need to know how to get unemployment benefits after unexpectedly losing a job, how taxes work (from your tax bracket to what tax credits you're eligible for), and how your ability to take out loans is impacted by your credit. Understanding these monetary terms (and many more) is necessary to living a financially fulfilled life, and sometimes it helps to have these terms explained in a way that makes sense.

That's where *Personal Finance in Plain English* comes in. Here you'll find more than 300 glossary terms that define and clarify any necessary personal finance language. After all, whether you're a seasoned pro or someone starting to improve your financial literacy, sometimes an easy-to-understand explanation to guide or teach you is exactly what's needed—which is why each glossary term is so simple to follow. First, each term is quickly summarized. Then, the "What it is" section provides a clear definition. Next, the "How it works" section further contextualizes and explains the concept. Finally, the "How it is used" example uses the term in an everyday sentence.

Throughout the book, you'll find the glossary terms grouped into common personal financial categories that will help you understand each term in context. For example:

- **Chapter 2: Income and Net Worth** includes terms like *1099, gross pay,* and *salary.*
- **Chapter 3: Budgeting and Financial Planning** provides definitions for *50/30/20, automatic payments,* and *envelope method.*
- **Chapter 5: Savings** has lingo like *APY, CD,* and *simple interest.*
- **Chapter 8: Credit Cards** includes *APR, grace period,* and *rewards.*
- **Chapter 12: Investing Terms** gives you words such as *bond, Nasdaq,* and *returns.*
- And there are plenty more!

Ultimately, whether you need a refresher on insurance or want to know what terms to use when meeting with your financial advisor, *Personal Finance in Plain English* will help you understand the complexities of your financial life and more. Using this book, you can take confident steps to build wealth, successfully navigate the investment arena, and effectively protect the economic future you're working so hard to create. The clear information in this book will help you manage your personalized financial goals easily and successfully.

CHAPTER 1

Common Banking and Financial Services Terms

Almost every part of your financial life will be touched by banking and financial services. After all, these services are connected to everything from savings to spending to borrowing to investing (which are topics covered in the chapters to come). Having a thorough understanding of this monetary lingo will give you a solid foundation to set you on the path of creating sustainable financial security.

This chapter will help you understand different types of financial institutions (like how banks differ from credit unions), the different players who operate in this arena (like financial advisors), and how the different types of accounts (like savings or checking) work. You'll learn which fees to watch out for and how to avoid them, the different ways to send and receive money, and what you need to know about using debit and credit cards. Read on to learn more!

ACH (Automated Clearing House) transfer

a secure way to send and receive money electronically

What it is: a system that allows for electronic fund transfers between banks and credit unions over the Automated Clearing House network

How it works: ACH transfers work sort of like emails but for money. The money is sent from one financial institution and is passed through the ACH to the receiving financial institution. Examples of ACH payments include direct deposit of a paycheck, online bill pay, and using Venmo or Zelle. ACH transfers are quick, safe, and usually free. Some banks may limit the amount you can send via ACH transfer in a single transaction or over a period of time (like a daily limit).

How it is used: Madeline sent her dog walker $25 by making an **ACH transfer**.

ATM (automated teller machine) fees

costs of using an ATM

What it is: an amount of money charged by financial institutions when you use ATMs to do your banking

How it works: ATMs are almost everywhere, and all you need is a debit card to withdraw cash from them. When you use an ATM that is owned and operated by a bank where you have an open and active account, you are using an "in-network" ATM.

ATMs that are owned and operated by a different bank or by an independent business are considered "out-of-network." In-network ATMs typically waive fees for their account holders. Out-of-network ATMs typically charge fees for transactions, with an average of $3.15 per transaction. Your bank may sometimes charge a separate, additional out-of-network fee (usually between $1 and $2). With a single ATM transaction, you may be charged almost $5.

How it is used: Donna paid $4.50 in **ATM fees** when she got cash from the ATM in the convenience store.

available balance

What it is: the amount of money in your bank account that's available for immediate use

How it works: Your bank account balance includes all the money you've put into it minus all the money you've taken out. Some transactions post immediately, but others may take time to be fully processed. Those are called pending transactions, and they affect your available balance, which is the amount of money you can withdraw from the account immediately. Your available balance may be less than your actual balance. Only the available balance can be used to make purchases, pay bills, or take withdrawals. Knowing your available balance can help you avoid overdraft fees and declined transactions.

How it is used: Lorena had $800 in her checking account, but her **available balance** was $600 due to pending transactions.

bank service fees

What it is: one-time or regular costs charged by banks and pulled directly from your account

How it works: Banks make money by charging their customers for services. When you open a savings or checking account, the bank may impose fees, even if the account is supposedly "fee-free." Some of these fees can be avoided by keeping a minimum balance in your account. Common bank service fees include:

- **Monthly account maintenance:** a charge just for having an account, ranging from $0 to $20 per month
- **Overdraft:** a charge imposed if you don't have enough money in your account for a transaction, but the bank allows it to go through anyway
- **NSF (non-sufficient funds):** charged when the bank declines a transaction because there's not enough money in your account
- **Returned deposit:** a charge applied when you deposit a check that bounces

How it is used: Gina was frustrated by **bank service fees** eating away at her account balance.

broker

intermediary between a buyer and seller

What it is: a professional who facilitates transactions for a fee

How it works: Brokers help make sure that purchases, sales, and trades go smoothly for all involved parties. Many industries, especially those with complex transactions, rely on brokers. Those industries include finance, investing, insurance, and real estate.

Brokers generally must undergo extensive training and licensing before they can perform services. For example, investment brokers (like stockbrokers) must pass the Series 7 exam before they can buy and sell securities. They earn money by charging commissions for every transaction they make.

How it is used: Shawna contacted a **broker** when she wanted to sell some shares of stock.

brokerage account

a place to hold investments

What it is: an account you can use to buy, sell, and keep a variety of investments including stocks and mutual funds

How it works: When you're ready to invest, you must open a brokerage account with a licensed broker. You deposit money into the account and then instruct the broker when you want to make investment transactions. Most brokerage accounts exist online, and you can order transactions online as well. These investment accounts can be used to trade or hold many different types of securities, including stocks, bonds, mutual funds, and exchange-traded funds.

There are three basic types of brokerage accounts: full service, discount, and robo-advisor. Full-service brokerage accounts cost the most to maintain but offer a wider range of services, including financial advisors who help manage your investments. Discount brokerage accounts work well for people who want do-it-yourself (DIY) investing, and they offer pared-down services and lower fees. Robo-advisor accounts make all investment selections based on algorithms and typically trade only mutual funds and exchange-traded funds.

How it is used: Amy opened a **brokerage account** online when she was ready to start investing.

cash equivalents

securities that can be turned into cash fast

What it is: a class of cash-like accounts and investments that can be sold or redeemed for cash immediately

How it works: Cash equivalents are typically held by large companies and can indicate strong financial health. These low-risk assets have maturities (meaning they've reached their end date) within 90 days and can be converted into cash right away. Examples of cash equivalents include certificates of deposit (CDs), money market accounts, commercial paper, and Treasury bills. When investors consider buying stock in a corporation, the company's total cash equivalents show how easily it can pay its bills and debts while still earning returns on those funds.

How it is used: When Aisha compared companies to invest in, she chose the one with more **cash equivalents** on the books.

checking account

money accessed for daily use

What it is: a bank account that allows easy access to funds for withdrawal in a variety of ways

How it works: Checking accounts are flexible deposit accounts at financial institutions, like banks or credit unions, that allow for frequent deposits and an unlimited number of withdrawals (assuming there's money to withdraw from). These accounts are used for daily spending and paying bills. The money can be accessed in many ways, including checks, debit cards, and ACH transfers. Checking accounts generally don't pay interest and come with a variety of bank fees, such as monthly maintenance fees and overdraft fees.

How it is used: Grant used his **checking account** to pay his rent, car payment, and credit card bills.

commission

payment for performing a task

What it is: compensation received once a transaction or service has been successfully completed, often tied to sales made or goals met

How it works: Commissions are extra forms of compensation usually tied to job performance and used as an incentive to increase productivity, and they're generally related to sales. They can be based on criteria like items sold, dollar amount of sales, items produced, and number of deals signed. Commissions can be straight or graduated. *Straight* refers to a single percentage, and *graduated* refers to an increasing percentage as specific goals are met and exceeded. Commissions may be paid in addition to or instead of salary.

On the personal side, investors pay commissions when they buy and sell investments through a broker. That can incentivize human brokers/advisors (as opposed to DIY online investing) to encourage more trades or to prioritize recommending particular securities. This can sometimes be a gray area, as brokers may be tempted to trade more to make higher commissions.

How it is used: Daniela got a straight 25% **commission** on every new laptop she sold for the electronics shop.

credit transaction

money added to a bank balance

What it is: an increase in an account balance when money is deposited or otherwise added to the account

How it works: From a banking perspective, a credit transaction represents money flowing into an account. That can include mobile deposits, direct deposit (of a paycheck, for example), cash deposits, ACH transfers into the account, vendor credits, and refunds. In a savings or interest-bearing checking account, any interest earned would be a credit to the account. These transactions are considered credits from the bank's point of view because they technically owe you the money in your account. When your balance increases, the bank's liability increases too.

How it is used: When Lucy deposited $500 into her savings account, she saw the **credit transaction** appear on her bank statement.

credit union

not-for-profit financial institution

What it is: like a bank in most ways, but owned and operated by the people—called members—who use its services

How it works: Credit unions work like financial co-ops, where every member-customer owns a piece of the institution. They offer many of the same services as banks, including checking and savings accounts, certificates of deposit, credit cards, and loans. Credit unions prioritize customer service and satisfaction, typically offer better interest rates than traditional banks, and charge fewer and lower fees than banks. However, credit unions usually have fewer physical locations, fewer ATMS, and more limited services and offerings.

To do any sort of business with a credit union, even if it's a one-time thing, you must become a member. In the past, only people in a specific group (like government employees) could join a credit union, but many are now open to anyone. You must open an account to become a member, though account opening requirements are generally minimal ($5 or $10 in many cases).

How it is used: Mike joined a **credit union** to get a better rate on his mortgage.

debit card

a way to spend money from a bank account

What it is: a payment method that pulls money directly from the linked bank account

How it works: Sometimes called bank cards, debit cards attach to specific bank accounts, usually checking accounts. They can be used to make purchases similarly to how credit cards are used, but they pay out immediately rather than creating a debt. Debit cards can also be used to get cash back during purchase transactions or to withdraw money from an ATM. For most transactions, debit cards require a personal identification number (PIN) to be entered, though some purchases may be made without that step. Because the debit card is connected to a bank account, spending is limited to that account balance. Debit cards may also come with daily spending limits. Debit card transactions may be subject to bank fees such as ATM fees and overdraft fees.

How it is used: Annie always uses a **debit card** for purchases to avoid running up credit card debt.

debit transaction

money subtracted from a bank balance

What it is: a decrease in a bank account balance when money is spent, withdrawn, or otherwise removed

How it works: From the bank's perspective, a debit transaction refers to money moving out of an account. That can include purchases, debit card transactions, automated bill payments, check payments, withdrawals, and bank fees. All of these debit transactions reduce the balance in the account, so it's important to be aware of them to avoid overdrawing from the account. Excess debit transactions can result in additional bank fees, which decrease the balance even further.

How it is used: Dan kept track of the **debit transactions** in his account to make sure he didn't spend more than he had.

depositor

person putting money in the bank

What it is: anyone who puts money into an account at a financial institution

How it works: A depositor is someone who stores money in a bank or credit union for safekeeping and possibly to earn interest. Technically, depositors allow the bank to use their money while it's in the bank's possession. In exchange, the bank pays interest to the depositor on the balance of funds in their account and provides some protection against loss.

Additionally, the FDIC (Federal Deposit Insurance Corporation) guarantees deposits of up to $250,000 per depositor, per bank, and per account category. For example, a depositor might have accounts at two different banks with $250,000 in each, and their full $500,000 would be covered by the FDIC. Credit unions have a similar guarantee through the NCUA (National Credit Union Administration).

How it is used: Elliott became a **depositor** when he opened his first checking account with $250.

financial advisor

professional money coach

What it is: an expert at helping people with personal finance issues such as investment, retirement, and debt management

How it works: Financial advisors help people create financial goals along with detailed plans to meet those goals. They can assist you in managing your own finances or take over aspects of it for you. Depending on your needs, the financial advisor can provide many services like helping you build an emergency fund, creating a budget, or choosing investments. They may also coordinate with other necessary professionals like tax preparers and estate planners.

Since a financial advisor will be intimately involved in your finances, it's important to choose someone you feel comfortable talking with about your financial issues. Check the credentials and references of any advisor you intend to hire, preferably one who serves as a fiduciary, meaning they are legally required to act in your best interests.

How it is used: Jake and Amy hired a **financial advisor** to help them figure out their financial goals and the best ways to achieve them.

joint account

account with two or more owners

What it is: a bank or investment account owned equally by two or more people, all of whom have full access to it

How it works: Joint accounts work like regular savings, checking, and investment accounts where anyone named on the account has full access to the funds. Account owners don't have to be related or in a personal relationship. In most cases, any individual owner can make transactions, but some may require all parties to sign off.

Joint accounts can be beneficial for people who want to combine assets or share expenses, parents who want to teach their children about financial responsibility, and people helping their aging parents manage their finances. Joint bank accounts are covered by the FDIC for up to $250,000 per owner. These accounts also come with some drawbacks, such as joint responsibility for all bank charges and fees, creditors may be able to attach the account (meaning, put a legal claim on it) based on the debts of only one owner, and all owners can see all transactions (there are no private transactions).

How it is used: Samantha and Carter opened a **joint account** to share household expenses when they moved in together.

NSF (non-sufficient funds)

bank account without enough money

What it is: a check written out for more money than your checking account balance

How it works: Non-sufficient funds (NSF) status indicates a checking account that doesn't have enough money in it to cover all of the pending transactions. It's applied when a check or other withdrawal transaction (like autopay) exceeds the account balance, the check is bounced (not paid out by the bank), and an NSF fee is charged by the bank. Single NSF fees can run as high as $35, depleting the account even further.

Staying on top of the account balance can help avoid NSF status and fees. People often forget about autopay bills or underestimate account fees, for example, which can lead to an overestimation of the balance and writing checks that exceed it. Check the balance online or through a banking app before making payments to make sure there's enough cash to cover transactions.

How it is used: When Rosa paid her rent by check, she didn't realize there wasn't enough money in the account and ended up in **NSF** status.

overdraft

spending more than you have

What it is: when the bank covers a transaction that you don't have enough money to cover

How it works: Sometimes people take more money out of their bank accounts than they have, and the bank covers the difference as an overdraft. This puts the account into a negative balance where the account holder now owes the bank money (like a loan). The bank charges an overdraft fee for this and may continue to charge fees and interest if the balance isn't restored to positive. Overdrafts can be caused by withdrawals, debit card transactions, bill payments, bank fees, and any other transaction that reduces the money in the account.

Some banks offer overdraft protection services. These work by linking another account that can be tapped into if the main account gets overdrawn, preventing the embarrassment of returned items or declined transactions. Banks typically charge for this service and may still charge fees related to the overdraft.

How it is used: Pam's checking account suffered an **overdraft** when her rent check and student loan payment came in before her paycheck was deposited.

transfer

moving money

What it is: sending funds from one bank account to another

How it works: Transfers involve moving money between different bank accounts. The accounts can be in the same bank or different banks, even in different countries.

There are three types of transfers: bank transfers, ACH transfers, and wire transfers. Bank transfers typically refer to moving money between your accounts at the same bank (like from your savings account to your checking account). These transfers happen immediately. ACH transfers are a (usually) free way to transfer money between different banks through a clearing system, which can take a few business days. Wire transfers are direct transfers (avoiding the clearinghouse) between different banks or other financial institutions, so they happen very quickly, usually within 24 hours. Wire transfers come with fees.

How it is used: Every month Gina makes a $100 **transfer** from her checking account to her savings account.

wire transfer

fast way to send money between banks

What it is: an expedient but costly way to move money from one bank to another

How it works: Wire transfers move money electronically and directly between accounts at different banks, often between two different account owners. These transfers can be domestic or international, offering a safe option for people who need to send money out of the country. The wire sender initiates the transfer and supplies all of the necessary information for the receiving bank account.

Wire transfers can be sent through banks or nonbank services, the most well-known of which is Western Union. It costs money to send wire transfers, and the fees are included in the amount of money transferred. Fees can range from around $10 to $50 per wire transaction, and in some circumstances, institutions may waive wire fees.

How it is used: Amelia sent a **wire transfer** to her daughter in college to make sure the money she needed arrived by the next day.

withdrawal

taking out money

What it is: pulling money out of a bank account

How it works: Any time money is removed from a bank account, it's considered a withdrawal, and these transactions reduce the account balance. Common checking and savings accounts allow unlimited withdrawals, but other types of accounts may limit the number of withdrawals made over a specific period. For example, money market accounts (not the same as money market funds) may limit customers to six withdrawals per month.

Some withdrawals may come with bank penalties or tax consequences. For example, withdrawing money from a certificate of deposit (CD) before its maturity will result in early withdrawal penalties. Withdrawals from IRAs (individual retirement accounts) are taxable and may also be subject to early withdrawal penalties.

How it is used: Raymond took a **withdrawal** of $100 cash to use at the water park.

CHAPTER 2

Income and Net Worth

As soon as you enter the workforce, you'll be earning income and building up your net worth. These two critical parts of your financial life seem like they should be straightforward, but they come with plenty of twists and confusing language. This chapter breaks down important ideas including the financial ins and outs of working for an employer. You'll learn about the differences between gross and net pay, why correctly completing your W-4 matters when you start a new job, and what to do if you're unable to work. There are many ways to earn income, and not everything requires trading time for money, so you'll also learn about passive income.

All forms of income funnel into your net worth, which helps you see where you currently stand financially. This chapter explains the different pieces that make up net worth, how to calculate it, and why it matters as you strive to create financial security.

1099

tax form for nonwage income

What it is: a group of annual information forms that report various types of taxable income

How it works: IRS (Internal Revenue Service) Forms 1099 contain details about income received during the previous year. This income must be reported on the recipient's annual income tax return. Even if a taxpayer doesn't receive a 1099, the income they earned must still be reported by law. These forms must be delivered to recipients by January 31 annually.

There are more than a dozen versions of Form 1099, including 1099-NEC (for nonemployee compensation for freelance or contract work), 1099-INT (for interest earned), 1099-DIV (for dividends earned), 1099-B (for brokerage transactions when investments are sold), 1099-G (for state and local tax refunds), 1099-K (for payments received from a payment platform like PayPal, credit card companies, and other payment processors), 1099-MISC (for rents, royalties, prizes, and other miscellaneous income), 1099-R (for distributions from retirement accounts), and 1099-S (for real estate transactions like selling your home).

How it is used: Kevin received three different **1099s** for his freelance work as a graphic designer.

assets

things you have

What it is: items of value that you own and could sell for cash

How it works: Assets are objects and resources you own that have financial value and could be converted to cash. Some assets, such as investments, may grow in value over time. Others can produce income while you own them, like rental properties and interest-bearing accounts.

Assets can be grouped into categories such as tangible (physical assets like furniture) and intangible (nonphysical things like shares of stock) or liquid (easily converted to cash) and illiquid (difficult or time-consuming to sell). Examples of personal assets include cash and cash equivalents, investments, retirement accounts, real estate, jewelry, vehicles, household goods, electronics, and collectibles.

It's good practice to keep an inventory of your assets, for both planning and insurance purposes. For planning, knowing your available assets can help with decision-making and financial management. High-value assets, whether individually (like a car) or collectively (like household contents), can be insured against loss.

How it is used: Li didn't realize that his Star Wars collectibles and classic guitars counted as **assets**.

direct deposit

money straight to your account

What it is: an electronic transfer of money directly into a bank account

How it works: Getting a direct deposit into your account makes the funds available right away, as opposed to waiting for a check to clear. Direct deposits are typically used for payroll, tax refunds, retirement account distributions, and various government benefits (like Social Security and unemployment).

Direct deposits offer several advantages over receiving checks. First, you don't have to deal with waiting for a check to arrive or for it to clear in order to get your money. Second, you don't have to visit the bank or use a mobile app or ATM to deposit the money; it just appears in your account. Third, electronic transfers are safer because there's no risk of a check being lost, damaged, or rejected (due to illegibility or incorrect information).

How it is used: Eleanor set up **direct deposit** for her paycheck when she started her new job.

earned income

pay for work

What it is: money received in exchange for performing labor or services

How it works: Earned income involves actively trading your time and labor for money or other compensation. Earned income includes salaries, wages, bonuses, commissions, tips, and self-employment earnings. In the US, this income type is more heavily taxed than unearned income and is taxable on two levels. First, you pay income taxes to the federal government and possibly one (or more) state and local governments. Second, you pay employment taxes on these earnings to cover Social Security and Medicare taxes.

With federal income taxes, earned income matters because it affects certain tax items. For example, you must have earned income to make contributions to an IRA (individual retirement account) and to qualify for the earned income tax credit (EITC).

How it is used: Janet had **earned income** from both her regular job and her side gig.

equity
what you fully own

What it is: the monetary value of all owned assets minus any outstanding liabilities

How it works: Equity in personal finance refers to how much money you would get if you sold an asset and paid off any related debt. One of the easiest examples to use is a home. The real estate is the asset, the mortgage is the liability, and the difference between the two is the equity. It represents the portion of the house that the homeowner actually owns.

When the value of assets increases and when liabilities are paid down, equity increases. But if asset values decline or debt increases, equity decreases. Equity matters because it represents the amount of money you would have left over if you liquidated all your assets and paid off all your debts. In some cases, equity can also be used as collateral for new loans, such as home equity loans.

How it is used: Shawn and Gus increased their **equity** by making extra mortgage payments during the year.

gross pay
earnings before deductions

What it is: total compensation before any money is withheld for taxes and other payroll deductions

How it works: Gross pay equals full salary or wages, such as $75,000 per year or $25 per hour, based on the agreement between the employer and employee. It's the starting point for every regular paycheck, regardless of the pay period. For example, an employee earning $75,000 per year who gets paid twice a month would have gross pay of $3,125 per paycheck. An employee earning $25 per hour who worked 40 hours during the pay period would have gross pay of $1,000 for that paycheck. Employment taxes—Social Security and Medicare—are based on gross pay.

How it is used: Jody's **gross pay** for her first job was $1,000 a week, and she was surprised that her actual paycheck was for much less than that.

liabilities

what you owe

What it is: debts you owe to people or institutions that have loaned you money

How it works: Liabilities represent money borrowed that must be paid back. They can include various types of debts including short-term or long-term, revolving or fixed, interest-bearing or interest-free, and secured or unsecured. Examples of liabilities include credit card debt, student loans, and mortgages. When liabilities exceed the resources available to pay them, that can cause financial problems and make it harder to cover monthly expenses.

Liabilities can also be used strategically to help build up personal financial stability and wealth over time. For example, taking out a mortgage to buy a house can lead to increased assets as the value of the house increases while the loan amount decreases.

How it is used: When looking at her full financial picture, Dominique made a list of all of her **liabilities** to see how much she owed altogether.

liquidity

how fast you can get cash

What it is: a measure of how easily something can be converted into cash

How it works: Liquidity refers to how easily an asset can be turned into cash without losing value. It's a measure of your financial resources and how quickly they can help you access money when you need it. For example, money in a checking account is highly liquid: available immediately for the exact amount of your balance. Your house, on the other hand, could take weeks or months to sell, involves many costs that reduce the amount of money you receive, and may not be sold for the price you want.

Liquidity matters because it controls whether you can pay all your living expenses and bills on time every month and how well you could weather an unexpected financial emergency.

How it is used: Having high **liquidity**, like cash in the bank and quick-selling assets like stocks, makes it easier to get through a sudden financial crisis.

net pay

take-home pay

What it is: earnings from work after taxes and deductions

How it works: Gross pay (or total pay) is the starting point for the money an employee receives in a paycheck. Many items get deducted from that total, some mandatory and others optional. Mandatory deductions include withholding for state and federal income taxes, employment taxes, and wage garnishments (due to a court order). The amount deducted for income taxes is based on information the employee submits on Form W-4. Optional deductions include things like retirement plan contributions, health insurance premiums, and Flexible Spending Account (FSA) contributions. Net pay equals gross pay minus all applicable deductions and may be substantially less money than gross pay.

How it is used: Elena's gross pay was $50,000 per year, but her **net pay** was closer to $32,000.

net worth

personal equity

What it is: the difference between total assets owned and total debts owed

How it works: Net worth is a picture of a person's current financial situation and stability. It's calculated by subtracting total debts (liabilities) from total assets, with the difference being net worth. It's a good benchmark for tracking financial progress over time.

Net worth can be negative, which is common for people just starting out on their personal financial journeys. Negative net worth indicates that a person has more debt than they could pay off with their current resources. Positive net worth shows that a person has more than enough resources to meet their debt obligations and would have money left over if they paid everything off. What matters most is that your net worth changes over time, moving from negative toward positive and then continuing to grow.

How it is used: Keisha's **net worth** was negative right out of college, but after she had worked for a few years, it became positive.

passive income

money without labor

What it is: money earned in a way that doesn't involve sustained active effort

How it works: Passive income comes from sources that require at most minimal work. In some cases, there may be initial work involved to set up a passive income stream but then none required to keep it flowing. Examples of passive income include interest, dividends, capital gains, rental income, and other investment income.

Passive income streams that involve up-front work include things like receiving royalties for writing a book, earning revenue from affiliate marketing and online ads on your website, and publishing an online course. Having passive income can help supplement earned income (from working) or even replace it.

How it is used: Norah invested in dividend stocks to create a **passive income** stream.

salary

compensation for work

What it is: amount paid to an employee for a specific period regardless of hours worked

How it works: Salary is the fixed amount an employee earns every pay period. It's normally paid biweekly or monthly and is typically referred to as an annual amount. Unlike wages, salary is consistent and predictable, and it doesn't depend on hours worked, so you always know how much you're going to get paid.

While salaried workers have historically been ineligible for overtime pay, the rules expanded eligibility starting July 2024 thanks to a rule enacted by the Biden administration: People earning less than $844 per week ($43,888 per year) will qualify for overtime, and that will increase to $1,128 per week ($58,656 per year) starting July 1, 2025.

How it is used: The starting **salary** for Kayla's new job was $60,000 per year.

self-employment income

working for yourself

What it is: earning money through work without an employer

How it works: People who work as independent contractors, freelancers, or sole proprietors rather than working as employees for a company or government entity are considered self-employed. Self-employment comes with many advantages such as being your own boss, setting your own hours, and deciding which projects you want to take on. Disadvantages include less predictable income, no paid days off, and no access to workplace health insurance or retirement plans unless you create them.

People who are self-employed are also responsible for proactively paying taxes, rather than having them withheld from a paycheck. Because self-employment income counts as having a business for tax purposes, you can deduct business expenses and reduce the amount of taxable income. Self-employment earnings are subject to both income and self-employment taxes, which can significantly increase an annual tax bill. Self-employed individuals are responsible for making quarterly estimated tax payments.

How it is used: Carmen earned $1,500 a month in **self-employment income** from her side gig.

SSDI (Social Security Disability Insurance)

disability money

What it is: monthly payments for people with health conditions that limit their ability to work

How it works: SSDI is a federal program that provides financial support for people with a recognized disability. Eligibility for the program is based on age, work history, and documented disability. The definition of disability here is very strict. The disability must have lasted or be expected to last for at least a year or result in death, make you unable to work at your previous job, make it impossible to adjust to other work, and prevent you from working at a "sustainable gainful activity" (SGA) level. In other words, you can't possibly support yourself. The Social Security Administration decides whether applicants are eligible, and, on average, only about 31% are initially approved each year. To learn more about the program, whether you might qualify, and how to apply, visit the Social Security website at www.ssa.gov/disability.

How it is used: Emily struggled with anxiety disorder and panic attacks, which made it hard to hold down a regular job, so she applied for **SSDI**.

SSI (Supplemental Security Income)

financial safety net

What it is: basic financial assistance for people with minimal income and resources

How it works: SSI is a federal program administered by Social Security. Eligibility depends on age, ability to work, income, and financial resources. Unlike SSDI, SSI benefits don't depend on work history. Limited income here means a single adult earning less than $1,971 per month (for 2024) and having total financial resources (such as money in a savings account) of $2,000 or less. To learn more about SSI or apply for benefits, visit www.ssa.gov/ssi.

In most states, people receiving SSI automatically qualify for Medicaid. In some states, SSI recipients may also automatically qualify for state-based support such as food or utility assistance. On average, between 35% and 40% of initial SSI applications are approved.

How it is used: Because of her disability, Gina was struggling to keep a job and had no savings, so she applied for **SSI**.

unemployment benefits

temporary cash when you're out of work

What it is: government-based compensation for people who have lost their jobs

How it works: Unemployment benefits are provided to people who get laid off or downsized, and sometimes to people who get fired or quit their jobs (depending on the circumstances). This joint state-federal program supplies income to jobless people as they look for work. It serves to partially replace lost income until new employment is obtained, and recipients are required to apply for jobs or undergo job training programs. States control the requirements and claims for unemployment. Most states offer this financial safety net for up to 26 weeks or until a new job starts. Unemployment benefits are not automatic when you lose a job; you must apply through the state program where you worked (if this is different than where you live) and wait for your application to be approved.

How it is used: After working at his job for 6 years, Gary got laid off and had to apply for **unemployment benefits** so he could pay his bills.

W-2

year-end tax form from employer

What it is: a summary of your total pay and taxes paid for the year from an employer

How it works: Employers complete Forms W-2 Wage and Tax Statements and distribute them to employees. The forms include the information needed to prepare a tax return, including total wages, taxable wages, tip income, federal and state income taxes withheld, and Social Security and Medicare taxes withheld. They also include information about other deductions from paychecks such as retirement plan contributions and health insurance premiums, as well as amounts your employer paid on your behalf like dependent care benefits. By January 31 each year, employers are required to provide W-2s to their employees who have earned at least $600.

How it is used: Jamie downloaded her **W-2** from her employer's payroll portal so she could file her taxes.

W-4

employee tax paperwork

What it is: an IRS form that tells your employer how much tax to withhold

How it works: Whenever you start a new job, you'll have to complete IRS Form W-4, Employee's Withholding Certificate. The form gives your employer important information like your Social Security number and helps them figure out how much federal income tax to withhold from your paycheck each pay period. The amount they withhold is sent to the IRS on your behalf throughout the year. At tax time, the IRS gives you credit for all of these tax payments. If you've paid too much, you'll get a refund. If you haven't paid enough, you'll owe more taxes.

Filling out the form requires information like your filing status, number of dependents, expected tax deductions and credits, and other types of income you may receive. Your W-4 should be updated any time there's a change in your tax situation. That could include things like getting married or divorced, having or adopting a child, working a second job, or starting a side gig.

How it is used: Jason had to fill out Form **W-4** when he started his new job.

wages

hourly pay

What it is: the amount of money paid to an employee based on the number of hours worked for the pay period

How it works: Wages are paid based on an hourly rate and number of hours worked. For example, someone earning $15 per hour who worked 40 hours during the pay period would earn $600. These employees are covered under the Fair Labor Standards Act unless they are specifically exempted. Hourly workers are entitled to receive overtime pay of 1½ times their normal pay rate (also called time and a half) when they work more than 40 hours in a week. The federal minimum wage is $7.25 per hour, but state minimum wages vary. For example, the minimum hourly wage is $11.00 in Arkansas, $14.00 in Illinois, $7.25 in North Dakota, and $16.00 in California.

How it is used: Priya's new job as a customer service rep paid **wages** of $22 per hour.

CHAPTER 3

Budgeting and Financial Planning

Thinking about budgeting and financial planning might make you nervous, but they're two of the most important steps for a lifetime of financial comfort. Budgeting isn't only pinching pennies and depriving yourself. Financial planning isn't only about retirement or picking investments. The truth is that both budgeting and financial planning involve making intentional choices about how to use your money and build up a secure nest egg. These tools help you design your ideal financial life, whatever that looks like for you. When used effectively, they help take the stress out of money management. First, you need to know how to assemble and use the tools properly in ways that work for you.

In this chapter, you'll find a breakdown of different budgeting styles, learn about how diversification and asset allocation can help you build wealth, and meet the professionals who can help you get where you want to go financially. Plus, you'll learn about resources you can tap into when you need assistance—everybody needs help sometimes.

50/30/20

What it is: a common way to divide up monthly income

How it works: The 50/30/20 budget is a method used to allocate your monthly take-home pay based on the following formula: 50% for needs, 30% for wants, and 20% for savings. The bulk of that income goes toward needs, which include things like rent or mortgage payments, utilities, minimum debt payments, healthcare, childcare, and groceries. The "wants" category includes optional expenses like entertainment, gym memberships, eating at restaurants, and other extras. The 20% allocated for savings could go toward building an emergency fund, contributing to an IRA (individual retirement account), making bigger debt payments, or investing.

The 50/30/20 rule is a guideline meant to help you get better control over where your money is going each month. It offers a simple way to manage your budget and prioritize essential expenses while setting you up for greater financial security.

How it is used: Jeanine tried the **50/30/20** budget method to get her spending under control.

asset allocation

investment buckets

What it is: dividing investments among multiple types of assets

How it works: Asset allocation refers to investing in many different types of assets to spread out risk. Different types of assets include things like cash, stocks, bonds, real estate, cryptocurrency, and precious metals, and they all perform differently based on the same market conditions. The theory behind this is that owning a variety of investments is less risky than putting all your eggs in one basket. For example, if all your investments are stocks and the stock market crashes, you'll lose more money than if you also had invested in gold and real estate.

Deciding on asset allocation must take into consideration your financial circumstances, risk tolerance, and timeline. Optimal asset allocations can change over time and should be revisited annually to make sure the existing allocation still works for you.

How it is used: Max's 401(k) had a 90/10 **asset allocation** with 90% in stock funds and 10% in bond funds.

automatic payments

recurring withdrawals for bills

What it is: preset regular transfers from a bank account

How it works: Automatic payments (also called auto-pay) allow you to set up regularly recurring bills to be paid on a schedule every month. Though these work best for predictable bills like rent, loan payments, and subscriptions, they can also be used for bills that can vary every month like utilities and minimum credit card payments. You can also set up automatic payments to transfer money to savings or investment accounts.

Advantages of automatic payments include never missing a due date for a bill, avoiding late payment charges, and not having to think about bills. Downsides can include the potential to overdraw your bank account, possibly giving a creditor direct access to your bank or credit card account, and not paying attention to your finances.

How it is used: Bridget set up **automatic payments** for all of her regular bills to make her life easier.

budget

money plan

What it is: a financial strategy for income and expenses

How it works: Budgets are tools you use to ensure your money is going where you want it to go. Creating a budget is a proactive way to track income and manage expenses for greater financial control and security. There are many ways to budget, and the best method is the one you can stick to. Budgets are meant to be flexible and adapt to your current goals and needs.

Working with a budget can ensure that all your bills get paid, allow you to afford wants, and put you on a path toward building wealth. When you have a plan for your money, you'll be able to reach your financial goals more easily.

How it is used: When she realized she wasn't sure where all her money was going, Candace created a **budget** to help control her spending.

CFP (certified financial planner)

licensed money advisor

What it is: a professional who helps people with all aspects of their financial lives

How it works: CFPs hold special licenses earned through extensive education, years of experience, and successfully passing rigorous exams. They have expertise in several areas including taxes, financial planning, retirement, estate planning, and insurance. A CFP designation ensures the professional is a fiduciary, meaning they are legally required to always act in the client's best interests. CFPs are bound to act according to the CFP Board standards for professional conduct, which includes proactively reporting everything from customer complaints to government inquiries to bankruptcies.

CFPs may charge an hourly fee (which averages around $250 per hour) or a full financial plan preparation fee (which can range from $1,500 to $3,000). When you meet with a CFP, they will ask many questions, analyze your current financial situation, listen to your financial goals and concerns, and work with you to create a plan that suits your needs.

How it is used: Anna and Paul hired a **CFP** to help them plan for saving for retirement and putting money into their kids' college funds.

diversification

wide variety

What it is: holding many different investments to minimize risk of loss

How it works: Diversification involves having a lot of different investments in a portfolio to help manage risk without sacrificing returns. It works hand in hand with asset allocation, taking risk reduction a step further. A portfolio would first be diversified among different asset classes such as stocks, bonds, and cash. For the next level, the stock portion of a portfolio could be diversified to hold dozens of individual companies; all of these would be stock investments but might include a mix of different industries and different company sizes.

How it is used: Kevin wanted **diversification** in his 401(k) plan investments, so he chose multiple stock funds with different strategies.

envelope method
cash stuffing

What it is: setting aside money for each monthly expense in advance

How it works: The envelope method was designed as a cash-based budgeting system whereby physical envelopes held the cash that could be used to pay for specific expenses. Once that cash was used up, either no more money could be spent in that area until the next month or money had to be taken from another envelope, reducing the amount available for that expenditure. The system works by requiring mindful spending to help people who struggle with financial control.

First, total monthly income is taken from all sources to calculate the money available. Subtract major essential expenses like rent or mortgage, loan payments, and utilities. The remaining funds are split among expense envelopes, used for items (such as groceries, household items, and gifts) where you can decide the amount you want to spend. Fill each expense envelope with the predetermined cash amount, which can be spent until it's used up.

How it is used: Marie had a hard time sticking to her budget using apps and credit cards, so she decided to try the **envelope method**.

essential expenses
costs of survival

What it is: things you need to pay for to exist and cannot live without

How it works: Essential expenses refer to costs that cover your necessities—the bare-minimum things you need to get by. While core essentials are generally the same for everyone, your necessities may differ from someone else's depending on your circumstances. Essential expenses always include food, clothing, shelter, necessary medical care, utilities (like phone and Internet), and transportation (to get to work or school).

Depending on your specific situation, they may also include costs to maintain a vehicle, childcare, pet care, and minimum debt payments. In a financial crisis situation, these are the expenses that must be covered for you and your family to survive. They include the bare-bones version of these items. For example, food includes groceries but does not include takeout, restaurant meals, and food delivery services.

How it is used: Erin prioritized **essential expenses** in her monthly budget, making sure her income was at least enough to cover those costs.

fiduciary

trusted professional

What it is: a professional bound by law to act for your benefit

How it works: A fiduciary is a professional who is legally and ethically obligated to act in the best interests of someone other than themselves. This designation can be especially important when hiring people to help manage financial issues, as they'll have access to a great deal of personal information and possibly direct access to bank or investment accounts. For example, a tax preparer will need your Social Security number, tax forms (like W-2s and 1099s), and banking information to complete your income tax return.

Different types of fiduciaries include certified public accountants (CPAs), certified financial planners (CFPs), and attorneys.

How it is used: Raymond faithfully upheld his **fiduciary** responsibilities as a CFP, always working to ensure his clients' financial well-being.

financial goals

lifetime money map

What it is: clearly defined ideas of what you want to do with your money

How it works: Financial goals set a framework for your monetary plan and how to achieve it. To successfully work toward and achieve financial goals, they need to be specific, measurable, achievable, realistic, and time-bound (SMART). The more defined the goal, the more likely it is to be met. For example, a financial goal could be to build a $2,000 emergency fund within 4 years by saving $500 per year ($42 per month). By setting clear goals, you'll be able to measure progress toward them, rework them if circumstances change, and transform financial ideas into reality.

How it is used: The only **financial goal** Linda and Juan could agree on was saving up $20,000 for a house down payment over the next 7 years.

fixed expenses

exactly recurring costs

What it is: expenses that stay the same every month

How it works: Fixed expenses are consistent and predictable, making them easier to budget for. At the same time, people generally have less control over these expenses, and they're harder to change. Examples of fixed expenses include rent or mortgage payments, loan payments, childcare costs, insurance premiums, subscriptions, and Internet fees.

Though fixed expenses remain stable, they can change periodically. For example, rent payments and insurance payments may change annually, but after annual adjustments, the following monthly expenses would be fixed. It's more difficult to affect a fixed expense, but it can be done through actions like changing providers, refinancing a loan, or moving to a different home.

How it is used: Angela's biggest **fixed expenses** were rent and health insurance premiums, and they took up most of her take-home pay every month.

inflation

price increases

What it is: widespread price growth over a period of time that affects the cost of living

How it works: Inflation measures how much average prices rise over a specific time period. These increases cause consumers' purchasing power to decrease, meaning it costs more money to buy the same goods and services, even though they haven't changed. Every dollar is worth less than it used to be during inflationary periods.

Inflation can affect every part of your financial life, from rent hikes to growing grocery bills to higher gas prices. When wages don't keep pace with consumer prices, people will have less (possibly no) discretionary income. That can make it harder to make ends meet and may lead to decreased savings and increased debt.

How it is used: Inflation was so high that Kara's weekly grocery costs had nearly doubled over the past year.

Lifeline

low-cost phone and Internet

What it is: a federal program that provides communication assistance to low-income individuals and families

How it works: Lifeline offers discounted pricing on monthly wired or wireless phone and Internet services to low-income families. The discount (as of 2024) is up to $9.25 per month per household off monthly broadband or bundled services, with additional support of up to $25 for individuals living on Tribal Lands. The program was introduced in 1985, expanded to cover cell phones in 2005, and updated to cover broadband Internet services in 2016. People can apply for Lifeline using the National Verifier application system on the USAC (Universal Service Administrative Company) website at www.usac.org.

How it is used: Blake and Brian applied to the **Lifeline** program to help them afford their monthly Internet bill.

LIHEAP (Low Income Home Energy Assistance Program)

energy assistance

What it is: a federal program that subsidizes energy costs for low-income individuals and families

How it works: LIHEAP is a federally funded program designed to help low-income households stay warm during the winter and cool during the summer. It helps families manage the costs of heating, cooling, energy, and home weatherization (such as insulation). Though the program is federal, it's administered at state and local levels. Applications for assistance are processed by the states or counties. Eligibility for the program, which is based on income, varies by locality. You can find out if you're eligible for LIHEAP assistance and where to apply in your area by visiting www.liheap.org.

How it is used: LIHEAP helped Ron and Amy avoid getting their power shut off when they couldn't afford their utility bill.

PYF (pay yourself first) rule

prioritize savings

What it is: a consistent way to build financial security

How it works: With the PYF rule, a portion of income goes directly into savings or investments, making it unavailable to pay expenses. The purpose of PYF is to prioritize saving and building wealth rather than funding them with leftover money (if there is any). PYF can be used to fund retirement plans like 401(k)s with contributions deducted directly from a paycheck. It can be used to divert a portion of direct deposit into a savings account.

How it is used: Tina used the **PYF rule** to transfer $50 to a savings account every time she got a paycheck.

Section 8

housing vouchers

What it is: financial assistance for low-income families to afford safe, private places to live

How it works: Section 8, also called housing choice vouchers, is a federal program designed to aid disabled people, elderly people, and low-income families who can't otherwise afford rent. The program is overseen by the US Department of Housing and Urban Development (HUD). Section 8 recipients are not required to live in subsidized housing projects. Rather, they can choose any home that meets the program requirements (such as safe and sanitary living conditions). Payments are made directly to landlords by the public housing agencies (PHAs) for the area, and the tenants pay the balance. Eligibility for Section 8 is based on income, family size, age, and disability status. Applications are handled by local PHAs. You can learn more about the program, including PHA contact information, at www.hud.gov.

How it is used: Paulo and Josh were afraid they'd lose their **Section 8** assistance when they moved, but they were able to use the housing vouchers at their new place.

SNAP (supplemental nutrition assistance program)

government food support

What it is: a public program designed to help low-income families buy food

How it works: SNAP is the primary anti-hunger program in the United States, providing food support for more than 42 million Americans. Also called food stamps or EBT (Electronic Benefits Transfer), SNAP funds come on a card (like a debit card) that can be used only to buy groceries or food-producing plants or seeds. It can't be used for things like personal care products, vitamins, pet food, diapers, or cleaning supplies. SNAP is a federal program that's administered by the states. Eligibility is based on gross and net income (after deducting certain essential expenses), assets, and work requirements. You can apply for SNAP through your home state's program. If you are eligible, the state will inform you about your benefit amount and certification period (how long you can receive benefits). More information about SNAP can be found at www.fns.usda.gov/snap.

How it is used: Chrissy received $174 in monthly **SNAP** benefits, which helped her afford groceries.

TANF (temporary assistance to needy families)

unrestricted government support

What it is: cash provided to needy families to cover a variety of essential living expenses for a short period of time

How it works: TANF gives financial support to families in crisis, helping them pay for basic survival expenses for up to 5 years. Unlike other programs, TANF allows this money to be spent on anything, such as rent or mortgage payments, utilities, and groceries. This program is federally funded and run by the states, and you apply for it through your state. Each state runs its program independently and may call it a different name. (It's called Temporary

Family Assistance in Connecticut and Temporary Cash Assistance in Maryland.) Along with cash benefits, states' TANF programs may include assistance with job training, work assistance, and childcare.

TANF eligibility varies by state and depends on factors like employment status, income, age, and dependent children. The program generally imposes work requirements on recipients, which can include a variety of work-related activities such as having a job, getting job skills training, or actively seeking a job.

How it is used: After she was laid off, Darlene applied for **TANF** to assist with childcare so that she could look for a new job.

time value of money

worth more now than later

What it is: the economic concept of a dollar today being worth more than a dollar in the future

How it works: The time value of money refers to the theory that a dollar you have now is worth more than a dollar you'd receive later on. This is because you can invest the current dollar and grow it, while the future dollar will be worth less due to inflation. Given the option between receiving $5,000 now or 3 years from now, it's more financially sound to take the $5,000 now even though they are the same amount of money. Today's $5,000 has more time to earn additional money through compounding and more purchasing power. The delayed payment represents missed opportunities and decreased relative value (even though the actual value is identical).

How it is used: Gina gave her grandkids each $10,000 when they turned 21 rather than making them wait for a future inheritance because of the **time value of money**.

variable expenses

costs that change

What it is: costs that differ from month to month, making them harder to predict

How it works: Variable expenses can be hard to budget for, as they can change from month to month. They vary because of price changes, different amounts purchased, or purchase frequency. While you can't control price changes, you may be able to control how often you buy things, how many you buy at once, or which things you buy. Common variable expenses include things like gas, groceries, dining out, entertainment, home utilities (gas and electric), gifts, clothing, and personal care items.

Though you can't necessarily predict variable expenses, you can track them and create reasonable estimates based on past spending.

How it is used: Diana tracked her monthly spending so she could get a better handle on her **variable expenses**.

WAP (Weatherization Assistance Program)

help with home energy efficiency

What it is: a federal program that provides a variety of ways to help homes use less energy and save on energy costs with updates and repairs

How it works: The WAP aims to reduce energy costs for low-income households through weatherization services. Funded by the US Department of Energy, this program serves an estimated 35,000 households every year, leading to an average of $372 in annual energy cost savings. The program is administered through the states, and households apply through their state weatherization administrator. Eligibility is based on income.

WAP starts with a whole-home energy audit, identifying inefficient areas and appliances. Weatherization services may include dozens of upgrades and repairs such as air sealing, installing insulation, replacing refrigerators with energy-efficient models, repairing or replacing gas venting systems, mold and moisture testing and elimination, cleaning/repairing/replacing home cooling or heating systems, and installing storm doors and solar window screens. You can learn more about applying for WAP at www.energy.gov/wap.

How it is used: WAP helped Emily's family save nearly 40% on their home energy bills with improved insulation and a new energy-efficient hot water heater.

WIC (Special Supplemental Nutrition Program for Women, Infants, and Children)

What it is: food supplied to low-income women and children whose nutritional needs wouldn't otherwise be met

How it works: WIC provides nutritious foods to mothers (including pregnant women) and children up to 5 years old. Many WIC clinics also offer nutrition education and counseling and may help refer clients for additional government services they may be eligible for. WIC is a federally funded program administered by the states. Eligibility is based on income and family size.

Participants may receive special debit-like cards or vouchers that allow them to buy specific foods or get them delivered. WIC-approved foods include things like infant formula, vitamin C–rich fruits and juices, milk, eggs, cheese, vegetables, and whole-grain breads.

How it is used: Katy and her two toddlers were able to get eggs, fresh fruit, and vegetables regularly by participating in **WIC**.

zero-balance budget

What it is: a financial plan where every dollar of income is assigned a specific job

How it works: A zero-balance budget aims to account for every dollar of income every month, tightly controlling where each of those dollars goes. It doesn't mean that every dollar gets spent. Rather, it predetermines how each dollar will be used, which may include saving, debt paydown, or investing. This budgeting method doesn't pull from the past to see how money has been spent but looks to the future to determine how money will be spent. Zero-balance budget (sometimes called zero-based budget) works well for people who want to prioritize savings or debt payments, avoid using credit cards, or approach spending more mindfully.

How it is used: Don took home $3,250 per month and used a **zero-balance budget** to allocate every dollar.

CHAPTER 4

Taxes

Thinking about taxes can make you anxious, confused, or frustrated. Income taxes in particular may seem upsetting because there are just so many rules! This chapter breaks down the biggest parts of the income tax return and tax calculations so you can feel more confident preparing your taxes every year—and make sure you're not overpaying.

Income taxes are probably the first type of taxes people think of, but they're not the only taxes you're paying. In fact, taxes are probably your biggest monthly expense, even if it doesn't seem that way. But when you put them all together—income taxes, sales tax, gas tax, property tax, and so on—the total could be half of your income. Taxes are a part of daily life, but there are things you can do to reduce the amount you're paying. First, though, you need a solid understanding of the different types of taxes and how they affect your finances. Ultimately, this chapter navigates through the different taxes in your life so you can manage them more effectively.

above-the-line deduction

big tax break

What it is: special ways to reduce income on a federal tax return

How it works: Above-the-line deductions are adjustments that help reduce your total income in order to get your adjusted gross income (a number affecting many other potential deductions and tax credits on your annual income tax return). These deductions are more valuable than standard or itemized deductions (collectively known as below-the-line deductions) because they have a greater impact on the bottom-line taxes due.

Above-the-line deductions include a portion of self-employment taxes, self-employed health insurance premiums, deductible retirement account contributions, HSA (Health Savings Account) contributions, student loan interest, and educator expenses. These special deductions get reported on Schedule 1 (a summary form included in federal income tax returns), and the total moves up to Form 1040 to get to adjusted gross income.

How it is used: Elizabeth took **above-the-line deductions** for her IRA contribution and the student loan interest she had paid.

AGI (adjusted gross income)

important tax return number

What it is: total income minus specific deductions known as "adjustments to income"

How it works: AGI is a federal tax calculation that's used to determine your eligibility for many tax deductions and credits. AGI equals total income from all sources minus above-the-line deductions, and it gets reported on line 11 of IRS Form 1040.

AGI matters because tax credits and deductions are often subject to AGI limitations. For example, the American Opportunity Tax Credit (which offsets the costs of higher education) is only available to taxpayers with AGI less than $90,000 (or couples with AGI less than $180,000). AGI also affects the ability to make Roth IRA contributions, deduct medical expenses, and take advantage of many tax credits.

How it is used: Regina's **AGI** was $41,500, which made her eligible for several tax credits.

capital gains tax

tax on investments

What it is: a special federal tax imposed when people sell assets

How it works: Capital gains tax applies to profitable asset transactions. In other words, it applies when someone sells something, usually an investment, for more money than they originally paid for it. If an asset is sold for a loss, there's no tax on the transaction, and that loss can be netted against any capital gains.

A special capital gains tax applies to long-term capital gains (assets held for more than 1 year before they were sold). Short-term capital gains, on assets held for 1 year or less, are taxed at ordinary income tax rates. Long-term capital gains tax rates are more favorable than regular income tax rates, ranging from 0% to 20%, and the rate assessed depends on filing status and taxable income.

How it is used: Nadine sold stock for a $2,000 profit and had to pay **capital gains tax**.

earned income

money made in exchange for working

What it is: all the money you make by working for an employer or yourself (if self-employed)

How it works: Earned income is a tax term referring to any income received in exchange for work, typically subject to both income and employment (Social Security and Medicare) taxes. It includes wages, salaries, bonuses, net self-employment income, contract work, gig work (like driving for Lyft), selling products or services online, and income from a business you own. It does not include income from interest, dividends, capital gains, and rent. Earned income applies to certain tax-related issues, such as the ability to contribute to an IRA or take the earned income tax credit (EITC), both of which require the taxpayer to have income from employment.

How it is used: Because Martha had **earned income**, she was able to contribute to a Roth IRA.

filing status

your relationship situation for tax purposes

What it is: a designation of your personal relationship to be used for tax purposes that affects your total income tax bill

How it works: Your federal income tax filing status affects everything from the amount of your standard deduction to available tax credits to tax rates. There are five filing statuses: single, married filing jointly, married filing separately, head of household, and qualifying surviving spouse. Each filing status has its own standard deduction and tax rate tables, so choosing the right filing status has a big impact on your overall tax bill. Your filing status depends on a combination of your marital status on December 31 of the tax year and whether you have any qualifying children (or other dependents) in your household. The only truly optional filing statuses are married filing jointly and married filing separately, which give married taxpayers a choice between filing individually or as a unit.

How it is used: Anya's **filing status** was single because she was not married on December 31 and had no dependents living with her.

Form 1040

federal income tax form

What it is: the main form filled out and filed for annual federal income tax returns

How it works: IRS Form 1040, US Individual Income Tax Return, is the primary form individual (not business) taxpayers complete and file each year. It works like a summary for all income, deductions, credits, and payments used to determine whether taxes were overpaid or are owed. The form also includes identifying information for the taxpayer and everyone else included on that tax return, such as spouses and dependent children.

How it is used: Every year, Tamara filed her **Form 1040** with her tax software.

income tax

What it is: a percentage of annual earnings sent to the government in exchange for public services

How it works: Income tax is the primary source of revenue for the US government, levied on both individuals and businesses based on their annual earnings. Many states and localities also collect income taxes. The amount of tax each person owes is based on complex calculations of income, deductions, credits, exemptions, and tax rates.

Income tax is levied on a wide variety of income sources, including salary and wages, self-employment income, investment income, rental income, gambling winnings, and withdrawals from traditional retirement accounts. The total income tax due is calculated by multiplying the applicable tax rate(s) by taxable income.

How it is used: Janeesa owed additional money in **income taxes** even though she had money withheld from her paycheck all year.

itemized deductions

expenses that reduce taxes

What it is: specific spending that can be used to offset income for tax purposes

How it works: Itemized deductions include particular expenses that can be subtracted from adjusted gross income to lower taxable income. Most individual taxpayers have the option of taking the standard deduction or itemizing deductions and can use whichever method gives them the greater tax break.

The most common itemized deductions for federal income tax purposes include mortgage interest, up to $10,000 of state and local taxes (SALT), medical expenses exceeding 7.5% of adjusted gross income, and charitable donations.

How it is used: Rob and Luna bought a house last year, so they had more **itemized deductions.**

MAGI (modified adjusted gross income)

tax return calculation

What it is: a tax computation where specific items are added back to adjusted gross income

How it works: MAGI isn't on the tax return, but the IRS uses it to determine eligibility for certain tax preference items including deductions, credits, and the ability to contribute to Roth IRAs or make tax-deductible traditional IRA contributions. It also determines whether the taxpayer will be subject to additional taxes, such as the net investment income tax.

The MAGI calculation starts with adjusted gross income, then adds back items such as deductions taken for IRA contributions, student loan interest deductions, half of self-employment taxes, and losses on rental properties.

The items added back depend on the purpose of the MAGI calculation. For example, MAGI for determining IRA deductibility would differ from MAGI used to determine whether Social Security benefits are taxable. In many cases, MAGI will be very similar to adjusted gross income.

How it is used: Kathryn couldn't make Roth IRA contributions because her **MAGI** was too high.

marginal rate

income tax percent

What it is: the tax percentage applied to your last dollar of income

How it works: The US income tax system has graduated rates, where different levels of income called tax brackets are taxed at different percentages. Whenever a taxpayer hits a new level, their next income dollars are taxed at the new associated rate. As income increases, so do tax rates.

The marginal rate is the tax percentage applied to the last dollar of income, the absolute top rate for that taxpayer. Their entire income is not taxed at that rate, so the marginal rate only applies to the portion of income in that tax bracket.

How it is used: Brianna had a taxable income of $56,000, so her **marginal rate** was 22%.

property tax

land and building fee

What it is: a government levy on real property used to fund public services

How it works: Property tax generally refers to a fee on real estate from a state or local government, though some states also levy taxes on personal property (like cars). The tax is based on the value of the property, which is determined by the tax assessor—a professional who regularly analyzes and updates property values. Property tax rates vary widely by location. For example, Hawaii has the lowest rate at 0.27%, and New Jersey has the highest rate at 2.33%.

Property tax is generally the largest source of revenue for local governments. These funds are typically used to support public schools, road construction, fire and police departments, and libraries.

How it is used: Lydia was dismayed that her **property tax** bill increased due to rising market values for homes in her area.

sales tax

extra money when buying things

What it is: an additional state or local fee added to the price of goods and services

How it works: Sales taxes are calculated and collected at the time of purchase from the buyer of a product or service. Forty-five states plus the District of Columbia levy sales tax, and local sales taxes are assessed in thirty-eight states. Though the remaining five states don't charge sales taxes, one of them (Alaska) has some areas where local sales taxes are collected.

Rates differ widely among the states and localities. Louisiana has the highest average combined state and local tax at 9.56%, and Hawaii has the lowest (not including Alaska), at 4.50%. Tax bases, meaning which items are taxable versus nontaxable, also vary among the states. For example, while most states don't charge sales tax on groceries, some states have a special lower grocery sales tax rate, and others charge full sales tax.

How it is used: Caroline waited for **sales tax** holidays to buy school supplies every year to avoid paying sales tax on her purchases.

self-employment taxes

What it is: payroll taxes on profits earned by working for your own business or as a 1099 worker

How it works: Self-employment taxes include Social Security and Medicare taxes. Normally these taxes are split 50-50 between an employer and an employee, with each party paying 7.65%. Self-employed people are responsible for both halves, bringing the self-employment tax to 15.3% on business profits (sales minus expenses). Of that, 12.4% goes toward Social Security and 2.9% goes toward Medicare.

To calculate self-employment taxes, 92.35% of profits gets multiplied by the tax rate of 15.3%. The 92.35% accounts for the "employer's" half of the self-employment taxes (7.65%), which is not yet deducted from the profits. Because there's no withholding tax for self-employed individuals, these taxes must be remitted quarterly using estimated tax payments.

How it is used: Suzanne owed **self-employment taxes** on her freelance income.

standard deduction

What it is: a predetermined dollar amount any taxpayer can deduct from their adjusted gross income

How it works: The standard deduction allows every taxpayer to reduce their federal taxable income by a fixed amount depending on their filing status. Introduced in 1944 to make taxes easier, the standard deduction has changed from a percentage of income to a flat dollar amount that has changed through the years. The standard deduction allows all taxpayers to reduce their taxable income without having to save receipts or prove expenses. It also reduces the number of people who must pay taxes. On top of the standard deduction, there are additional deductions for taxpayers who are age 65 and older or blind.

How it is used: Marina used the **standard deduction** every year on her taxes because she didn't own a home or have high medical expenses to deduct.

tax

mandatory payment

What it is: money paid to a government entity by law

How it works: Tax is a form of government revenue that must be paid by its citizens. It can be imposed on a variety of things such as income, property, sales, estates, wealth, and businesses. Tax revenues are used to provide support and services to the public and can include such things as defense, healthcare, road construction and repair, and education. In the US, taxes are imposed at the federal, state, and local levels.

How it is used: When Bob added up the many types of **taxes** he paid, they were his largest budget expense.

tax bracket

income bucket

What it is: a range that determines the tax rate for a person's specific income

How it works: The federal income tax system is graduated based on income layers called brackets. Each bracket of income gets taxed at a specific rate, with the rates increasing as the income increases. When a taxpayer's income exceeds one bracket and enters a new one, only the excess income gets taxed at that next bracket's rate. There are seven federal income tax brackets, and the corresponding income tax rates range from 10% to 37%. Brackets depend both on income levels and federal tax filing status.

Here's an example of how tax brackets work. Suppose Ben was single and had $60,000 of taxable income. Based on the 2024 tax brackets (found at www.irs.gov), Ben would pay 10% on the first $11,600 ($1,160) plus 12% on the next $35,550 ($4,266) plus 22% on the remaining $12,850 ($2,827), and his tax bill would come to $8,253.

How it is used: Martha got a raise that pushed her income into the next **tax bracket**.

tax credit

What it is: a direct reduction of the amount of taxes owed

How it works: Tax credits are dollar-for-dollar reductions of tax that decrease the amounts owed in a similar way to payments. These credits are more advantageous than tax deductions, which lower taxable income, because they have a bigger impact on how much a taxpayer owes.

Examples of common income tax credits include the child tax credit, the earned income tax credit (EITC), education credits, the adoption credit, and the child or dependent care credit. Most of these credits are nonrefundable, meaning they can reduce your tax bill to zero but not below. Others are refundable, which means they can create a negative tax bill that will increase your refund.

How it is used: Eli ended up getting a bigger tax refund than expected because he was eligible for **tax credits**.

tax deduction

What it is: an expense that can be subtracted from income on a tax return

How it works: Tax deductions reduce taxable income, resulting in a lower tax bill. Some deductions are taken "above the line," meaning they're used to calculate adjusted gross income. Other deductions are taken "below the line," meaning they further reduce adjusted gross income to get to taxable income. For below-the-line deductions, taxpayers have the option of defaulting to the standard deduction or choosing to itemize deductions. The taxpayer may use whichever method results in a lower tax bill.

How it is used: Trish tried to take advantage of as many **tax deductions** as possible so she could get the biggest possible refund.

taxable income

What it is: total earnings minus all applicable deductions

How it works: Americans aren't taxed on 100% of their income. At the very least, they can subtract the standard deduction, which reduces the amount subject to taxes. In addition, they may be able to take above-the-line deductions or use itemized deductions, which can reduce taxable income even more.

Some forms of income are not subject to federal income taxes or may be exempt in certain circumstances. Examples of potentially nontaxable income include Social Security retirement benefits, gifts and inheritances, life insurance proceeds, qualified distributions from Roth IRAs, and municipal bond interest.

How it is used: Renee's total income was $62,000, but her **taxable income** was only $43,000.

CHAPTER 5

Savings

Financial security is having money available when you need it, and you need to have savings to achieve that. Building savings involves splitting part of your money from the rest and keeping it in a separate place for safekeeping. This chapter details everything you need to know about how and where to save your money. There's more to savings than most people realize, and choosing the wrong place to store your money can result in lost interest.

This chapter delves into the different kinds of savings accounts, their benefits and drawbacks, and when it makes the most sense to use them. You'll learn everything from money market accounts to 529 plans to high-yield savings accounts. You'll also find a breakdown of the different types of interest to ensure your money is working hard for you.

529 plan

What it is: state-sponsored, tax-advantaged savings accounts to be used for school spending

How it works: 529 plans were originally created as tax-advantaged college savings accounts for named beneficiaries. Money in the 529 plan can be used to pay for higher education costs at accredited institutions, tuition for K–12 education, and up to $10,000 of student loan debt. These plans are administered by the states, and state provisions vary widely.

There's no federal tax deduction for the contributions to a 529 plan, but there's no tax on the account earnings while they remain in the account. Money withdrawn from a 529 plan that is used to pay for qualified education expenses won't be taxed for federal and possibly state income tax purposes.

How it is used: Maria and Ari set up **529 plans** for each of their children to help offset their eventual college costs.

APY (annual percentage yield)

total yearly rate paid

What it is: the effective rate earned on savings or investments over a year, taking compounding into account

How it works: APY refers to the amount of interest earned on a bank account for 1 year converted to a percentage. It can differ from the interest rate, which is the percentage applied to calculate interest on the account. APY can be used to refer to either simple or compound interest. The interest rate will equal the APY for simple interest, but it will differ for compound interest.

For example, for a simple interest account with $5,000 earning 5%, the annual interest earned would be $250 and the APY would be 5% ($250/$5,000). For a compound interest account with $5,000 earning 5% compounded quarterly, the annual interest earned would be $254.73 and the APY would be 5.095%. A higher APY means the money will grow faster. When comparing similar accounts, it can be financially advantageous to choose the one with the greater APY.

How it is used: When Lina was comparing online savings accounts, she chose the one with the highest **APY**.

balance

how much money you have

What it is: the total amount of money currently in a bank account

How it works: An account balance is the running total of the money put into and taken out of a bank account. Money deposited into the account, including any interest earned, increases the balance. Money withdrawn from the account, including any fees charged, reduces the balance. For interest-bearing accounts, the balance affects the amount of interest earned, and a higher balance results in more interest earnings.

Keeping tabs on the balance can help account owners track their finances as well as quickly detect any bank errors or identity theft issues. You can check an account balance at an ATM, online, or through a mobile banking app.

How it is used: When Carlos checked his **balance**, he saw that he had saved $350 of his $500 goal.

CD (certificate of deposit)

locked-up money

What it is: a savings account where money is unavailable for a set time

How it works: A CD is a type of savings account where a specific amount of money is kept for a predetermined amount of time. In exchange for the agreement to not withdraw the money before that time is up, the bank pays interest at a higher rate than on standard savings accounts. CD terms can range from 1 month to several years. Interest is paid at the end of the term when the CD is cashed out.

How it is used: Renata opened a 6-month **CD** at her bank because the interest rate was higher than on her savings account.

compound interest

What it is: earnings earned on previous earnings, allowing for faster financial growth

How it works: Compound interest means that interest gets paid both on the balance in an account and on any interest that's already been earned; the interest earns its own interest. This phenomenon greatly speeds the growth of money in an interest-bearing account.

Here's how it works. An account earning compound interest at a rate of 5% a year has a starting balance of $10,000. The first year, it earns $500, bringing the new balance to $10,500. The second year, it earns $525, bringing the new balance to $11,025. The third year, it earns $551.25, bringing the new balance to $11,576.25. Because of the compounding, the amount of interest earned every year increases even though the account owner hasn't added any additional funds to the account. And, in this example, the balance would double within 15 years from compounding alone.

How it is used: Charlie's savings grew quickly due to the power of **compound interest**.

deposit

What it is: money delivered to and held in an account in a financial institution

How it works: Depositing money at a bank or credit union increases the value of the account. In many cases, financial institutions require a minimum deposit to open an account. Deposits can be made with cash, checks, ACH transfers, and any other means the bank will accept.

There are two main types of deposits: time deposits and demand deposits. Time deposits (sometimes called term deposits) generally require leaving the money in the account for a set period, often in exchange for higher interest rates. The most common version of these are certificates of deposit (CDs), which typically come with terms between 3 months and 5 years. Withdrawing funds early from a time deposit can result in penalty fees or lost interest.

Demand deposits can be withdrawn at any time (on demand) with no consequences. Checking and savings accounts are both examples of demand deposits.

How it is used: Sharon made a **deposit** into her savings account when she got birthday money from her grandmother.

emergency fund

rainy day money

What it is: cash kept in a separate place to be used in times of crisis

How it works: An emergency fund is a pool of dedicated cash set aside to use in case of an unexpected expense or lost income. It provides more financial flexibility in times of crisis, which can help prevent the need to use credit cards or borrow money at high interest rates.

The optimal size of an emergency fund depends on your personal situation. Generally, it's a good idea to have at least 6 to 12 months' worth of essential living expenses in an emergency fund. However, any amount saved in an emergency fund can help cover unplanned financial events. Even putting a small amount into such an account regularly (such as $10 per month) can build up over time, increasing your resources and financial stability.

How it is used: Angela tapped into her **emergency fund** when her cat needed surgery and was able to avoid paying by credit card.

HYSA (high-yield savings account)

extra interest on banked money

What it is: a way to grow savings much faster than in a regular account

How it works: HYSAs offer significantly higher interest rates than traditional savings accounts, often 10 times as much or more. Typically offered by online-only banks, HYSAs give you the opportunity to grow your savings much faster. For example, a regular savings account may pay a 0.45% interest rate, while an HYSA pays 4.5%. Following that, the regular savings account with a $1,000 balance would earn only $4.50 in a year, while the same balance in an HYSA would earn $45.

How it is used: Sofia put her emergency savings into an **HYSA** so it could earn extra interest.

interest

money earning money

What it is: a payment received for keeping money in the bank

How it works: Interest is the cost of using someone else's money. With a savings account, the bank pays interest on the balance, which can change over time. Interest is typically expressed as a percentage rate that will be applied to the account balance at specified times during the year.

Banks do this because they can use the money in savings accounts (such as making loans with it) and pay you a fee for that. The interest you earn gets added to your account balance and is available for withdrawal.

How it is used: Zara put her money into a bank account so it could earn **interest**.

money market account

savings-checking combo

What it is: a bank account that combines features of both savings and checking accounts

How it works: Money market accounts are interest-bearing bank accounts that normally pay higher rates than traditional savings accounts. They typically allow money to be withdrawn by debit card and checks but limit the number of permitted withdrawals (usually to six) per month. They also tend to require larger opening deposits than standard savings accounts and may also require the depositor to maintain a minimum ongoing balance. These accounts offer a safe place to save large amounts of money, as they are offered by banks and are FDIC-insured for up to $250,000 (unlike money market *funds*, which are investments and not a form of savings account).

How it is used: Diego opened a **money market account** to hold the money he inherited to earn extra interest until he could decide how to invest it.

online savings account

electronic-only banking

What it is: money in a bank that has no physical location

How it works: An online savings account is generally accessed exclusively online, through apps, and through ATMs rather than at a walk-in bank branch. Online savings accounts typically offer higher interest rates than those at brick-and-mortar banks and often have fewer and lower fees. Customers can access their accounts and perform transactions any time, any day, and are not limited by traditional banking hours. Disadvantages may include having difficulty depositing cash and reaching human customer service representatives. If the online bank does not have or belong to an ATM network, customers may incur more ATM transaction fees.

Opening an online savings account is quick and easy. Once you've chosen a bank and an account, you can apply online or through the app by supplying some basic personal information. When the account is open, you can fund it by transferring money directly from another account or by depositing a check.

How it is used: Harry opened an **online savings account** because it had a higher interest rate.

simple interest

rate times balance

What it is: the easiest way to calculate interest for loans or savings

How it works: Simple interest is calculated by multiplying the original principal amount of a loan or savings account balance by the stated interest rate. The calculation does not include interest on accumulated interest. This can make loans easier to pay off because the interest doesn't get added to the principal before the next month's interest is calculated. On the savings side, though, it can slow wealth accumulation because you don't earn interest on previously earned interest.

For example, a $10,000 balance with a 5% annual interest rate would earn $500 per year. Only money deposited into the account would earn interest, and prior interest payments would not be included as part of the interest-earning balance.

How it is used: Shauna's savings account earned **simple interest**, so her balance grew more slowly than she had expected.

targeted savings

intentionally separated money

What it is: money put away and designated for a specific purpose

How it works: Targeted savings is a way to amass money toward achieving a financial goal. It can work better than a general savings account for planned expenditures, especially big-ticket items like new furniture or vacations. Using targeted savings can help you avoid going into debt to fund such items, sidestepping the "buy now, pay later" strategy salespeople often push. These accounts have the added benefit of earning interest while you work to achieve financial goals, allowing you to accomplish them faster.

How it is used: Adria set up a **targeted savings** account to fund a trip to Greece in 2 years.

traditional savings account

money in a physical bank

What it is: money deposited in a bank location the depositor can visit in person

How it works: Traditional savings accounts are offered by banks and credit unions with physical locations as a place for people to store money and earn interest. These accounts are protected by the FDIC, making them safe places to hold cash that's still easily accessible. Traditional savings accounts generally pay relatively low interest rates, averaging less than 1%. They can be a good option for keeping money for short-term needs or emergency funds. While traditional savings accounts are primarily offered by brick-and-mortar banks, they can also be found at some online banks.

How it is used: Gina set up **traditional savings accounts** for each of her kids so they could visit their money occasionally.

CHAPTER 6

Insurance

Nobody wants to have to pay for insurance—when nothing is going wrong, it feels like a waste of money. But insurance provides a financial safety net for bad times, and on top of dealing with some kind of emergency, you also risk losing a substantial amount of money. It covers excessive expenses that most people couldn't afford without draining their savings or taking on debt. There are many different types of insurance, and the kinds you need depend on your circumstances.

Insurance is one of the most complex and confusing topics in personal finance, so this chapter focuses on clearly explaining the different kinds of insurance, along with the language you need to know to fully understand how your policies work. In this chapter, you'll learn about some of the most important types of insurance and their features, including the difference between actual cash value and replacement cost, whether term or whole life insurance best fits a situation, what annuities are, and why you might need both long-term disability and long-term care insurance. It also includes everything you need to know about your policies, from deductibles to premiums to riders.

actual cash value

What it is: insurance coverage that reimburses for belongings less their lifetime wear and tear

How it works: Actual cash value (ACV) refers to how an insurance policy will reimburse you for losses: the original cost of the item less depreciation (decrease of value over time due to normal wear and tear). This coverage can save money on premiums because the insurance company won't have to pay out as much, but those payouts may fall short when you're trying to replace lost, damaged, or stolen property. For example, suppose you bought a laptop for $1,200 3 years ago and it's been destroyed by water damage. The insurance company says it's worth $900 now ($1,200 minus 3 years of depreciation), so that's how much you'd get reimbursed.

How it is used: Janine got **actual cash value** coverage with her homeowners insurance to save money on the premiums.

annuity

What it is: an insurance contract designed to provide steady income for a certain amount of time

How it works: An annuity is a type of insurance contract where the purchaser usually makes a lump-sum payment and receives a regular series of payments in exchange. Annuities are most frequently bought to provide steady income in retirement, like pension payments. Earnings on annuities (including interest, dividends, and growth) grow tax-deferred, which means you won't pay income taxes on them until you pull out the money. All the money you receive gets included in your regular taxable income.

Annuities can be set up in many ways with a wide variety of add-on features available, and the contracts can get complex and confusing. They can be immediate, where payouts begin right away after the purchase, or deferred, where payouts begin at a predetermined future date. The three main types are fixed, variable, and indexed, each referring to the way the annuity grows.

How it is used: Louis wanted to beef up his guaranteed retirement income, so he purchased an **annuity**.

auto insurance

car safety net

What it is: a contract that helps minimize financial losses for car-related incidents

How it works: Auto insurance is a contract between an insurance company and a person buying insurance coverage to protect them against losses related to their car. The insured person pays regular premiums to keep the insurance policy (the contract) in force. In exchange, the insurance company agrees to offset costs from accidents, vandalism, or theft. Most states require at least basic liability insurance for anyone owning and operating a vehicle.

Auto insurance policies typically cover damage to vehicles, bodily injury, and property damage. Exact coverage details will be spelled out in the policy and include such things as coverage limits and deductibles. Premiums are based on factors like age, gender, driving record, accident history, and history of moving violations (like speeding tickets).

How it is used: Bob got **auto insurance** when he bought his first car.

claimant

person getting insurance money

What it is: someone who requests money from an insurance company to cover a loss

How it works: A claimant is a person who files a claim (a formal request) for payment from an insurance company to offset a loss they've suffered. The claimant can be an insured person or someone harmed by the insured person, such as the other driver in a car accident.

The claimant must often submit proof to support their claim, which may include receipts, medical bills, and pictures of damages. Once the insurance company validates and approves the claim, they will release payment to the claimant according to the terms of the policy.

How it is used: Jenna acted as a **claimant** when she went to an out-of-network doctor and had to file a paper claim with her health insurance provider.

collision

crash coverage

What it is: insurance coverage for a car that is damaged after hitting something

How it works: Collision coverage is a type of add-on car insurance that protects against monetary loss when your vehicle has hit another car or object, like a tree or guardrail, or is damaged driving over a pothole. It covers the cost of repairing or replacing the damaged car, no matter who was at fault, as long as your car was being driven at the time. It's not usually required by state law but may be required for a leased vehicle (by the leasing company) or financed vehicle (by the lender).

How it is used: Dana had **collision** coverage on her car because it was one of the conditions of her car loan.

comprehensive

non-collision coverage for cars

What it is: optional auto insurance that covers losses from virtually everything except collisions

How it works: Comprehensive auto coverage protects against loss from events beyond the driver's control. It covers a wide variety of problems, including theft, vandalism, fire, windshield damage, damage involving animals (if the car hit a deer, for example), and acts of nature (like a tree falling on the car during a storm). The payout for comprehensive car insurance is generally limited to the value of the vehicle minus a deductible.

How it is used: Elena's **comprehensive** insurance kicked in when her car was damaged during a hailstorm.

deductible

What it is: required out-of-pocket payment made before insurance starts covering expenses

How it works: A deductible is the amount an insured person has to pay with their own money before the insurance company starts to pay. It's a standard feature with every type of insurance (except life insurance), though some policies will let the insured opt for a $0 deductible for additional premiums. Deductibles can apply per year or per incident, which is more common. Deductibles are normally fixed dollar amounts, but some types of policies may use percentages instead.

How it is used: After Monica paid the $2,000 **deductible** to her contractor, the costs to repair her basement were fully covered by her homeowners insurance.

good driver discount

What it is: reduction in car insurance costs for drivers who don't have any accidents or tickets

How it works: Good driver discounts, also called safe driver discounts, vary by insurance company but can involve up to 40% savings on auto insurance policies for drivers who have gone 3 to 5 years without having an accident or moving violation. Accidents caused by other drivers where the insured was not at fault don't count against them for good driver discount purposes. With some insurance companies, the discount may increase the longer the driving record remains clean.

How it is used: Pete's driving record helped him qualify for a **good driver discount**, and he saved $250 on his car insurance premiums.

health insurance

medical coverage

What it is: paid or reimbursed medical care costs according to an annual plan

How it works: Health insurance is a contract where the insured pays premiums in exchange for an insurer covering a portion of the costs of medical care. In the US, you can obtain health insurance through an employer's group health plan, the Health Insurance Marketplace (called "the exchange") created by the Affordable Care Act (Obamacare), private insurers directly, or the government as Medicare or Medicaid.

Health insurance can be difficult to navigate depending on the type of plan. For example, managed care plans, such as HMOs (health maintenance organizations), may cover only in-network providers (medical professionals who agree to accept specific insurance companies' plans). An insured person may be required to pay deductibles, co-pays, coinsurance, and out-of-pocket maximums, and they may pay thousands of dollars for healthcare costs before health insurance kicks in.

How it is used: Erin hadn't yet met her **health insurance** plan's $2,500 deductible, so she ended up paying for all of her healthcare costs.

homeowners insurance

house protection

What it is: coverage for damage to a home and its contents

How it works: Homeowners insurance helps cover financial losses from damage to a home and its contents, personal property theft, and liability. These policies generally cover four areas of loss, including exterior damage, interior damage, damage or loss of personal items, and injuries to people while they're on the property. Acts of nature, such as floods and earthquakes, are often specifically excluded from homeowners insurance policies and may need to be separately purchased for homes at risk.

Payments for homeowners insurance policies are often wrapped into monthly mortgage payments. The mortgage company takes responsibility for paying the premiums when they're due.

How it is used: Darlene and Eric filed a claim on their **homeowners insurance** when their family room was damaged by fire.

insurance broker

policy intermediary

What it is: a professional who helps people find the best policies to fit their needs

How it works: Insurance brokers act as intermediaries between insurance companies and people who need insurance. These experts specialize in the insurance industry and can help their clients sift through available options based on any criteria they choose. They can save you a lot of time and money, making sure you choose the right coverage and deductibles for your situation and take advantage of all applicable discounts. Insurance brokers work for their clients, not for the insurance companies, which helps prevent any potential conflicts of interest. They cannot write policies, but they deal with insurance agents to help their clients get the correct coverage.

How it is used: Anna was overwhelmed by all the homeowners insurance options, so she worked with an **insurance broker** to choose the best policy.

life insurance

financial support for your family

What it is: money paid to your family or other beneficiaries when you die

How it works: Life insurance is a contract between an insurance company and a person whereby the person pays premiums in exchange for an amount of money to be paid to their beneficiaries when they die. In the event of death, the insurance company will pay out death benefits to the named beneficiaries. There are two main types of life insurance: term, which lasts for a set number of years, and permanent, which doesn't expire as long as premiums are paid.

Life insurance can provide monetary support for people who depend on the insured person financially after they die. Life insurance proceeds are not taxable to the beneficiaries. Those proceeds can bolster financial security in a time of crisis, pay off debts or medical bills, or be invested for the future.

How it is used: Bonnie and Joe bought **life insurance** when their first child was born to make sure he'd be taken care of financially.

long-term care insurance

nursing home and home healthcare coverage

What it is: coverage for personal care assistance services during periods of disability

How it works: Long-term care insurance covers health-related costs that health insurance (including Medicare) does not cover, such as assistance with daily living activities, that will be needed for at least 3 months. This can include things like bathing, dressing, and getting in or out of bed for people suffering from chronic illnesses, disabling injuries, and other medical conditions. Most people will need these services at some point in their lives, often for 2 to 5 years.

Long-term care costs can be astronomical, ranging from $40,000 to more than $100,000 annually, and can quickly wipe out even well-funded nest eggs. Long-term care insurance policies subsidize those costs up to a predetermined limit. Premium costs increase with age, and it may be difficult to qualify for a long-term care policy after age 70 (the time when many people start needing this assistance).

How it is used: After seeing how much her mother's in-home care cost, Renata and her partner decided to get **long-term care insurance** policies.

long-term disability insurance

income replacement while you can't work

What it is: coverage that provides financial support to replace lost wages due to accident or illness

How it works: Long-term disability insurance (sometimes called LTD) replaces pay for workers whose earning ability is interrupted by illness or injury for extended periods. This insurance is often provided by employers as an employee benefit, but it can be purchased by individuals as well. The payouts help people pay for regular living expenses during the time they can't work.

According to Social Security, around 25% of Americans will experience a disabling event between age 20 and retirement. Disabling incidents include things like fractures and sprains, strokes, heart attacks, pneumonia, and pregnancy complications that can make it impossible to work. Long-term disability insurance typically kicks in between 90 days and 6 months after the disability began, and benefits can last for 2, 5, or 10 years (depending on the terms of the policy).

How it is used: Mara was grateful for her **long-term disability insurance** benefits after a car accident left her unable to work for a long time.

Medicaid

public health insurance

What it is: comprehensive healthcare coverage for low-income individuals and families

How it works: Medicaid is a joint federal-state program that provides free or low-cost health insurance to people with limited income and resources. Rules for eligibility vary by state, with some covering all people with incomes below a state level (expanded Medicaid) and others that also look at factors like family size, age, and disability. You can apply for Medicaid through your state program directly or through www.healthcare.gov.

Medicaid typically covers things like doctor visits, prescription drugs, hospital stays, emergency room visits, and pregnancy care. It may also assist with costs for transportation for medical services (when there's no other option), dental care, and eye exams depending on the state program guidelines.

How it is used: Ginny applied for **Medicaid** when she lost her job and health insurance.

policy

insurance contract

What it is: the agreement between the insurance company and the person buying insurance

How it works: A policy is a legal contract that specifies an agreement between an insurance company and the person (or business) being insured against potential losses. The insured pays a fee, called a premium, in exchange for protection from or reimbursement for costs arising from specific perils.

Insurance policies contain at least four essential pieces of information: premiums, deductibles, coverage, and policy limits.

The most common types of insurance policies include auto, health, homeowners, life, and renters insurance. Policies may also be written to cover more specific losses, such as identity theft or travel risks.

How it is used: Henry read through his car insurance **policy** to make sure he understood his coverage in case of an accident.

premium

cost of insurance

What it is: the money spent to keep an insurance policy active

How it works: Insurance premiums are the amount paid each period to buy an insurance policy. Premiums are determined by a combination of factors, including type of policy, coverage limits, deductibles, location, and risk factors. Risk factors (meaning things that increase the risk of a claim) could include age, claims history, driving record, or health history.

Premium payment frequency varies by type of insurance and policy arrangements. For example, a premium on an auto policy may be paid semiannually, and health premiums are usually paid monthly. Most insurers offer payment plans that convert premiums to monthly, such as paying monthly installments for a semiannual car insurance premium, for easier budgeting.

How it is used: Eddie paid $560 per month in health insurance **premiums**.

premium tax credit (PTC)

health insurance discount

What it is: a reduction in the cost of health insurance purchased through the Health Insurance Marketplace

How it works: The PTC is a dollar-for-dollar reduction in federal income taxes to help offset the costs of insurance bought on the exchange (the federal Health Insurance Marketplace). The amount of the credit is based on a sliding scale where lower-income individuals get bigger tax credits. When you enroll in your marketplace plan, you can let the system estimate your credit and reduce your premiums throughout the year (the advance premium tax credit, or APTC), or you can take the credit when you file your taxes. The PTC doesn't just reduce your taxes to zero and stop there; you can get it as a refund. If your financial circumstances change during the year, update your information in the marketplace, and your PTC will be recalculated. If you get the APTC, you could end up having to pay all or a portion of it back if your income increases during the year.

How it is used: Jaime and Estrella qualified for a **premium tax credit** and used it to lower their health insurance premium costs all year.

renters insurance

personal property protection

What it is: coverage for your possessions when you live in a rented space

How it works: Renters insurance offers financial protection for tenants who suffer losses due to circumstances like theft, burst water pipes, and fires. These policies primarily cover your belongings but may also cover things like medical bills, personal liability, loss of property while traveling, and temporary housing. Personal property coverage includes everything you own, from furniture to electronics to bicycles to dishes.

These policies are among the most affordable insurance policies, averaging approximately $150 annually (around $12.50 monthly). Like all insurance policies, premiums depend on a variety of factors, including deductibles, coverage limits, and applicable discounts.

How it is used: Doug got **renters insurance** when he moved into his first apartment.

replacement cost

the amount of money to buy a new one

What it is: insurance coverage that reimburses you for the current cost of items you've lost

How it works: Replacement cost coverage will provide you with funds to replace damaged or lost belongings with new ones, no matter the age or condition of the old belongings. The replacement cost is based on a similar property of the same type and quality. For example, suppose you paid $1,200 for a laptop 3 years ago, and it's been destroyed by water damage. A new laptop of similar quality now costs $1,800, so the insurance company payout would be based on that price. The insurance reimbursement comes in two parts: the actual value of the lost item at first, and then the difference once you prove (with receipts) that you've replaced it.

How it is used: Because Deanna had **replacement cost** coverage, she was able to buy all the things she'd lost after her place was robbed.

rider (endorsement)

extra feature

What it is: additional specific insurance coverage added to a policy for a fee

How it works: A rider, also called an endorsement, is an extra provision in an insurance policy that adds or changes coverage. It's normally used to cover a specific item that's not covered in the basic policy or that needs more coverage than the base policy allows. Riders can be tailored to the specific needs of the insured depending on their unique situation. They can be added to any type of policy for a fee on top of the regular premium. Common examples of riders include long-term care provisions added to a life insurance policy and special coverage for jewelry or art on a homeowners insurance policy.

How it is used: Anna got a **rider** on her renters insurance policy to cover her engagement ring and ruby earrings.

short-term disability insurance

work absence coverage

What it is: agreement to replace a portion of lost salary due to illness or injury for 3 to 6 months

How it works: Short-term disability insurance protects your earned income if you're unable to work due to an illness or injury; most policies include pregnancy coverage as well. It replaces a portion of your income so that you can continue to pay your bills while you can't work. Benefits typically replace 40% to 70% of income for up to 6 months, so actual payouts depend on your pre-disability earnings. This coverage is often provided by employers as part of a benefits package, but it is also available to individuals.

How it is used: Toby had **short-term disability insurance** through his job and used it when he missed several months of work following a car accident.

term life insurance

limited-time death benefit

What it is: a temporary life insurance policy that pays death benefits to named beneficiaries during a predetermined period

How it works: Term life is the most basic type of insurance policy. The insured pays premiums for a specific period in exchange for death benefits during that period. Term life policies typically last between 10 and 30 years, then expire. Death benefits are only paid out if the insured dies while the policy is still in force. That money goes to the beneficiaries tax-free and is meant to replace the income lost by the death of the insured.

How it is used: Dwight and Angela each took out 30-year **term life insurance** policies when their first child was born.

umbrella insurance

covers everything else

What it is: a policy that provides additional loss protection beyond the coverage of other policies

How it works: Umbrella insurance is designed to provide backup coverage if another policy (like homeowners or auto insurance) hits its limit. It can also protect against losses that aren't included or are specifically excluded from other policies. The umbrella policy kicks in once the primary policy payouts have been exhausted. It can also offer liability protection for people who participate in high-lawsuit activities, like renting a room in their house, coaching a kids' sports league, and having a pool or trampoline in the backyard.

How it is used: Rob and Lisa got **umbrella insurance** when their teenage son started driving.

VUL (variable universal life)

invested insurance

What it is: life insurance with a component that can be invested

How it works: VUL is a complicated, expensive whole life insurance policy where a portion of the cash value can be invested in accounts like mutual funds. This offers the opportunity to increase the cash value, but there is also a risk of losing money due to stock market downturns. If the cash value falls too low, premiums will be increased to keep the policy in force.

With VUL, the insured can decide how much to put into the policy every year, as long as it's enough to cover the annual premiums. The excess money goes toward cash value. The cash value portion, including the part that's invested, grows tax-deferred (like a retirement account). While the policy is in force, policyholders can access their cash value by borrowing from it or taking withdrawals.

How it is used: Graham worried about lost death benefits in his **VUL** when the investments he'd chosen performed poorly.

whole life insurance

death benefits with no time limit

What it is: a policy that pays out death benefits whenever the insured dies, as long as the premiums have been paid

How it works: Whole life insurance provides death benefits for the entire life of the insured, unlike term life insurance, which expires at a predetermined time. In addition to stated death benefits, these policies have a cash value component that earns tax-deferred interest at a fixed rate; the cash value is a key feature of whole life insurance. These are the most basic, lowest-risk permanent life insurance policies.

Most whole life policies have level premiums, so the cost is the same every month the policy is in force. A portion of premiums goes toward cash value, and that cash value percentage declines over time as policy costs increase with age. Cash value can be withdrawn or borrowed from by the insured at any time, though this may reduce the amount paid in death benefits.

How it is used: Annabeth took cash value withdrawals from her **whole life insurance** to supplement her retirement income.

CHAPTER 7

Borrowing Money and Establishing Credit

At some point, you'll probably need to borrow money. Whether you borrow through a credit card, a student loan, or a mortgage, it's important to understand the full impact that will have on your current and future financial life. Reading and understanding loan agreements can be difficult, but it's important to know exactly what's expected of you when you borrow money. That includes understanding some of the terms you'll find in this chapter, like *negative amortization*, *cosigners*, *debt-to-income ratio*, and *utilization*. You'll also learn about the difference between revolving and non-revolving debt, and what it means to be preapproved.

Most people don't think about their credit until they need to borrow money, and then they run into problems. Building strong credit will put you in a better financial position if you ever need a loan, no matter what kind or how big it is. This chapter details the components of a credit score, outlines a credit report, and explains what happens during a credit check.

amortization

What it is: the way equal loan payments are spread out over time to pay off the full balance with interest

How it works: Amortization is a method of calculating scheduled, equivalent loan payments that get applied to both loan principal and interest. The loan payments never change, but the interest and principal proportions of each payment shift over time. The interest portion initially accounts for most of the payment and decreases over time, and the principal portion increases over time. This type of payment is typically used for non-revolving debt like mortgage and auto loans, along with some personal loans. Amortized loans come with amortization schedules that include all the loan payments for the life of the loan, including the interest and principal breakdown for each.

How it is used: Dan received a copy of his **amortization** schedule when he signed the paperwork on his car loan.

balloon payment

What it is: an unusually large amount due at the end of a loan, generally the full remaining loan balance

How it works: A balloon payment is the final payment due on a loan that is structured as a much larger payment than the regular monthly amount. The earlier loan payments may be all or primarily interest payments, with the balloon payment used to pay off the entire loan, which is usually called a balloon loan. These may be used for business loans and occasionally for short-term mortgage loans—usually for people who can make large down payments. There are two main ideas behind this strategy. One is that the beginning payments are lower than they would be otherwise, helping borrowers with limited cash flow and the expectation that their income will increase substantially. The second is that they'll be able to refinance the loan before the balloon payment comes due.

How it is used: Sarita and Dante refinanced their home mortgage before the $200,000 **balloon payment** was due.

bridge loan

What it is: short-term financing used as a stopgap measure during a financial transition, often used when moving houses

How it works: A bridge loan helps bridge a financial gap experienced during a time of transition. These loans are most commonly used when someone is buying a new house while selling their old house and the timing doesn't work well financially. The bridge loan helps smooth out the cash flow during that type of situation where the money that would otherwise be used has been delayed. Bridge loans tend to come with high interest rates and short payback periods, typically no longer than 3 years.

How it is used: Mark and Patty had to get a **bridge loan** when the original buyers for their old house dropped out and they needed to close on their new home.

cosigner

What it is: a person who agrees to take on the full responsibilities of someone else's loan

How it works: Cosigners often come into play when a person with no or low credit needs to take out a loan. Lenders are cautious about getting their money back from that person, so they ask another person to agree to make the loan payments if the original borrower doesn't. Cosigners tend to be close friends or family, but that's not a requirement. They must, however, have excellent credit and the ability to make the loan payments. This reassures the lender that they will get paid and increases the chances for loan approval.

The cosigner faces two main risks with this arrangement. First, if the borrower doesn't make loan payments, the cosigner is legally responsible to do so. Second, if the borrower makes late payments or the loan goes into default before the cosigner steps in, it can negatively affect the cosigner's credit score.

How it is used: Caleb couldn't qualify for a car loan on his own, so he asked his mom to be his **cosigner**.

credit agency

monetary history analyzer

What it is: a company that gathers financial information about people and companies to determine how likely they are to pay back debts

How it works: Credit agencies collect information that helps them assess whether a person or a company can and will pay back any borrowed money and create reports with the data. The credit agencies then sell those reports to potential lenders to use in making their lending decisions. Individuals can also get copies of their own credit reports for free once a year.

The three major US credit agencies are Equifax, Experian, and TransUnion. While they report on similar data, their analysis and scoring policies differ, and what appears in one agency's report may not appear or may appear differently in another's report.

How it is used: Renee requested a copy of her credit report from each of the three major **credit agencies**.

credit builder loan

reverse borrowing

What it is: a way for people without an established financial history to create a positive one

How it works: Credit builder loans work the opposite way regular lending does. These loans help people with no or limited credit history establish good credit. While it's called a loan and acts like a loan, from the borrower's perspective, it works more like a savings plan. The loan payments are made first, and when the loan is paid in full, the lender releases the funds. Payments are reported to the credit agencies, helping the borrower build up a positive credit reputation. Many credit unions, community banks, and community development financial institutions offer credit builder loans, typically in amounts ranging from $300 to $1,000.

How it is used: When Susannah graduated college, she used a **credit builder loan** to develop a good credit score.

credit check

verification of ability to manage debt

What it is: an inquiry into your credit history by an entity deciding whether to lend money or enter into another type of financial agreement (like a lease)

How it works: Credit checks are performed by companies like lenders, landlords, and employers when they need information about your financial background as part of their decision-making process. They typically include reviewing your credit report, which often starts with a credit score, to assess your level of financial responsibility and reliability. Hard credit checks, which occur when you've applied for new credit, affect your credit score. Soft credit checks don't affect your score, and they occur when you or a potential employer check your credit or a credit card company preapproves you for an offer. Whenever you apply for credit, the application requires you to grant permission for a credit check.

How it is used: The apartment complex ran a **credit check** on Sam before approving her application.

credit limit

maximum borrowing

What it is: the cap on the amount of money that may be borrowed, usually connected to revolving debt

How it works: A credit limit is the largest amount you can charge on a credit card or line of credit (the two main types of revolving debt). The balance of the account changes over time, increasing when money is spent and decreasing when payments are made. At any given time, the balance cannot exceed the credit limit, though the lender can change the limit based on your payment history. Hitting the credit limit on a credit card is called maxing out the card, meaning it can't be used for additional spending until the balance is paid down or the limit increased. Credit limits are set by lenders based on the borrower's credit report and employment status.

How it is used: Josephina hit the **credit limit** on her credit card, so she couldn't use it for a while.

credit report
detailed financial history

What it is: a document that includes a person's long-term financial history used to determine their ability to make timely payments for a loan or lease

How it works: A credit report contains details of your financial history and includes things like current and former debts, payments, and defaults (late or missed payments, if any). It also includes personal identifying information like your name, address, and Social Security number. Most people have multiple credit reports, one from each credit agency, which may contain some differences in format and details.

The information that fills a credit report comes from credit card companies, lenders, and other creditors. Those creditors are not required to supply information to all three major credit agencies, which can account (in part) for differences among the reports. Everyone is entitled to a free copy of their credit report every year, which can be found at www.annualcreditreport.com. Reviewing your credit report can help you catch mistakes, which may include identity theft, and make sure they get corrected promptly.

How it is used: AnneMarie checked her **credit report** every year and usually found at least one mistake on it.

credit score
lendability rating

What it is: a number that indicates whether you will make debt payments on schedule

How it works: A credit score is a number that predicts how likely you are to pay back debts on time. The number summarizes your credit history in a single figure, so creditors can immediately determine your general creditworthiness. It's calculated using a scoring model, a formula developed by the scoring companies, based on several key factors including total current debt, history, how and which type of debts you have, length of your credit history, how much of your available credit is being used, and whether you've applied for any new credit.

Credit score users, such as lenders and landlords, often set minimum eligible credit scores for their applicants.

How it is used: Tariq tracked his **credit score** regularly to make sure it didn't drop too much.

DTI (debt-to-income ratio)

borrowing as a percentage of earnings

What it is: total monthly debt payments divided by total monthly income

How it works: Your DTI is a ratio that compares your total monthly debt load with your total gross (before taxes) monthly income. The monthly debt load includes things like loan payments, minimum credit card payments, and rent. For example, if you have $1,000 rent, $150 in monthly minimum credit card payments, a $350 car payment, and a gross monthly income of $3,000, your DTI would equal 50% (total debt of $1,500 divided by $3,000 income).

Lenders use your DTI to determine whether you'll be able to manage additional monthly debt payments. Most lenders prefer applicants to have a DTI of less than 36%, but some may go as high as 50% depending on the circumstances.

How it is used: Hoa and Alex worked on lowering their **DTI** of 44% before applying for a mortgage.

FICO score

commonly used credit rating

What it is: a 3-digit number that summarizes a person's creditworthiness

How it works: FICO scores, developed by the Fair Isaac Corporation, are credit scores that serve as summary snapshots of creditworthiness and are based on information found in your credit report. These scores help lenders make quick decisions when considering loan applications. FICO is the most commonly used credit scoring system, though several others exist.

FICO scores range from 300 to 850. Scores under 580 are considered poor, meaning extremely risky to lend money to. Scores of 580 to 669 are considered fair, 670 to 739 good, 740 to 799 very good, and over 800 excellent. People with high FICO scores tend to get better loan deals with better terms and lower interest rates.

How it is used: Amber was excited to see that her **FICO score** had increased to 675.

lien

property claim

What it is: a legal right to specific assets that can be seized and sold to settle a debt

How it works: A lien is a legal claim to assets. Liens can be established by creditors, judgments, and taxing authorities to satisfy unpaid debts. The lienholder may seize the assets named in the lien and sell them to collect the money they are owed. Liens can be voluntary, such as in the case of named collateral for a loan, or involuntary, such as the result of legal action or an IRS claim. Any kind of asset, including a bank account, can have a lien placed on it. You can remove a lien by paying the attached debt in full.

How it is used: When Charles and Norah paid off their mortgage, the mortgage company released the **lien** on their house.

loan

money to be paid back

What it is: agreement between a lender and borrower about how and when borrowed money will be repaid

How it works: A loan is a borrowed sum of money that is meant to be paid back with interest (extra money to make it worthwhile for the lender) according to a preset schedule. Loans generally fall into two main categories: revolving (money that can be re-borrowed as it's paid back) and non-revolving (a single fixed amount). Common loans include credit cards, mortgages, lines of credit, and student loans.

When someone needs money, they may apply to a financial institution for a loan. The institution (lender) decides whether the borrower is likely to pay them back using information such as credit score, credit report, and employment history. If the loan gets approved, the borrower and lender agree to terms (such as loan amount, interest rate, loan fees, payment schedule, and final payback date) and sign a contract detailing the agreement.

How It is used: Marisol needed a **loan** to buy her car because she didn't have enough money on hand to buy it outright.

loan balance

current amount of debt

What it is: the sum of money a borrower currently owes a lender

How it works: A loan balance is the remaining unpaid debt that a borrower owes a lender on a specific date. That balance is calculated by taking the original amount of the loan, subtracting any principal payments made, and adding any items that increase the balance (which might include fees, penalties, and interest). It's generally used to calculate interest; reducing the loan balance also reduces the amount of interest to be paid.

How it is used: Evelyn checked her **loan balance** periodically to track her progress toward becoming debt-free.

negative amortization

increasing loan balance

What it is: when interest gets added to a loan balance, increasing the amount due

How it works: Negative amortization occurs when payments on a loan aren't made or aren't sufficient to cover the interest due, and that unpaid interest gets added to the loan balance. Even when on-time full loan payments are being made, the loan balance can increase because of this phenomenon. Negative amortization happens most frequently with student loans and adjustable-rate mortgage (ARM) loans where monthly payments can end up being less than the monthly interest. In addition to increasing the loan balance, it increases the monthly interest (based on the loan balance), which can make the loan balance grow even faster.

How it is used: Negative amortization increased Stephanie's student loan balance every month, even though she was making her payments on time.

non-revolving debt

a loan with limits

What it is: a one-time loan for a specific amount of money that is paid back on a set schedule

How it works: With a non-revolving loan, you borrow a set amount at once, and the lender expects to be paid back according to a schedule. These loans are predictable, come with planned payments, and have predetermined payoff dates. Both parties know from the start when the loan will be paid in full. If you need more money, you must start the process again from the top and take out another loan. Examples of non-revolving debt include car loans and mortgages. In most circumstances, the outstanding balance of a non-revolving loan will only decline over time. (The exception is a loan with negative amortization, when unpaid interest gets added to the balance of the loan.) Non-revolving debt can be either secured or unsecured.

How it is used: The bank issued Emma a **non-revolving debt** for her new house, due to be paid in full in 30 years.

preapproved

already evaluated positively

What it is: a temporary green-light status given by a lender in advance of a potential borrower's application

How it works: Preapproved status is a preliminary assessment of someone who may apply to borrow money from a lender. It lets the potential borrower know that if they do apply for the loan or credit card, they are likely (not guaranteed) to be approved. Lenders frequently use notification of preapproved status as a tool to attract specific borrowers and entice them into applying. Sometimes the information pulled to make the preapproval determination will affect your credit score; these are called "hard" inquiries and are usually used to preapprove candidates for large loans like mortgages.

If you receive a preapproval notification, that does not mean you've been approved for the loan or credit card. It's a first step in the full application process, which involves a close look into your financial history.

How it is used: Tina and Marco were **preapproved** for several credit cards, but they only applied for the one with the lowest interest rate.

promissory note

IOU

What it is: a basic written agreement that serves as proof that one person owes another money and will repay it

How it works: The simplest loan agreements are called promissory notes. They include everything from an IOU tossed into a poker pot to a one-page, fill-in-the-blank form with simple payment terms. They may or may not contain specific time limits or payment amounts, but they do create a paper trail for the loan. However, these don't offer the same legal protections as a formal agreement. These are often on-demand loans, which means that the lender can call for repayment whenever they want as long as they provide reasonable notice.

How it is used: Joe gave his sister a **promissory note** when he borrowed money from her.

quotes

proposed loan terms

What it is: a way for borrowers to compare estimates from multiple lenders before deciding which to borrow from

How it works: Quotes let you see how much different lenders will charge you for the same loan, allowing you to compare them and decide which is best for your situation without a commitment to a particular loan. These estimates are normally associated with mortgages, and borrowers can request as many as they like from different lenders in exchange for the limited information necessary to create the quote. To get the most useful information, ask each lender for the same loan features and provide them with the same information when getting quotes.

One of the most important features is a rate lock, and not all quotes come with one. A rate lock means the interest rate specified in the quote is guaranteed for a specific period. Without that, the rate quoted could be different than the actual loan rate.

How it is used: Marina got five **quotes** before choosing a lender for her mortgage.

refinancing

replacing a loan

What it is: exchanging an existing loan for one with better terms

How it works: Refinancing helps borrowers improve the terms of a loan they already have by replacing it with a more favorable loan. It can be used to secure lower interest rates, change or extend a payment schedule, lower monthly payments, and more. Borrowers typically refinance when interest rates fall to save thousands of dollars over the lives of the loans. They may also refinance when their credit has improved, making them eligible for better loan terms.

This strategy is available for any kind of loan, but mortgages and student loans are often refinanced. The process involves working with the existing lender or a new lender and applying for a new loan. The loan proceeds pay off the existing loan, and future payments go toward the replacement loan.

How it is used: Thomas investigated **refinancing** his student loans after his credit score rose above 750.

revolving debt

money you can continually borrow

What it is: a set amount of money (credit limit) from which you can borrow as much or as little whenever you choose

How it works: Revolving debt is sometimes referred to as open-ended debt because you can borrow the same money repeatedly. Your balance due goes up and down depending on your financial activity, and your monthly payment amount varies based on the current outstanding debt. When you spend more of your available credit line, you owe more. When you make a payment, you owe less. Even though you can only borrow up to the maximum credit limit at any given time, you can borrow much more than that amount over time. Revolving debt can be secured, such as with home equity lines of credit (HELOCs), or unsecured, such as with credit card debt.

How it is used: Martha took on **revolving debt** throughout the month as she made purchases with her credit card.

utilization

used-up portion

What it is: the percentage of available credit currently being used

How it works: Utilization, also known as credit utilization ratio, shows how much you've borrowed out of the total amount you *could* borrow. It usually applies to revolving credit, such as credit cards and lines of credit, but it may include non-revolving credit. You need two numbers to figure out your utilization: the total balance of your outstanding credit and your total available credit. For example, if you had three credit cards and owed $1,000 on each and had a credit limit of $2,000 on each, your utilization would be $3,000 divided by $6,000, or 50%.

Credit agencies heavily incorporate utilization into your credit score, and lenders often look at utilization when making application decisions. Most consider a good utilization ratio to be below 30%.

How it is used: Renata didn't realize her **utilization** would increase when she closed an old credit card, and closing the account temporarily lowered her credit score.

CHAPTER 8

Credit Cards

Most people are exposed to credit cards before they have any idea how they work or how to use them properly. That can lead to significant amounts of high-interest-rate debt that feels impossible to pay off because when you pay by credit card, it may not feel like you're borrowing money. The idea of easily manageable minimum payments can make every purchase seem like a great bargain, and that mindset makes it easy to end up in debt. But if you know how credit cards really work before you start using them, you can turn them into tools that help you build up a credit history and improve your financial situation, rather than the other way around.

This chapter dives into the ins and outs of credit cards, providing clear insights into everything from annual fees and APRs to variable rates and over-limit fees. You'll learn how credit card interest gets calculated, how to take advantage of the grace period, and how to avoid getting caught in the minimum payment trap.

annual fee

cost of having a specific credit card

What it is: an expense charged by some credit card companies for the privilege of using a certain card

How it works: Annual fees are amounts you have to pay every year associated with specific credit cards. These fees can range from $95 to more than $500 yearly and are normally billed to the applicable credit card. They're charged in exchange for the benefits of being a cardholder, which may include cash back on purchases, airline miles, credit card reward points, purchase protection, and travel insurance.

While it may seem wise to avoid cards with annual fees, they can be financially advantageous if the benefits outweigh the fees. Card perks can save you money when they're tailored to your lifestyle, such as airline miles or hotel points for someone who travels extensively.

How it is used: Dani's credit card had a $350 **annual fee**, but she more than recouped that with the cash-back rewards she got on groceries.

APR (annual percentage rate)

full cost of borrowing

What it is: a percentage representing all yearly interest and fees paid on a credit card, often used for comparative purposes

How it works: The APR on a credit card includes all the costs of borrowing, interest, and fees the cardholder would pay in 1 year if they carried a balance. The total costs are converted to a percentage, the APR, for ease of comparison with other borrowing options. APRs can vary widely by cardholder credit score, with lower credit scores resulting in higher rates. APRs can be fixed or variable depending on the underlying interest rate.

Though often used interchangeably with interest rate, APR includes more fees than interest alone, so it's a better reflection of the total cost to carry the card. For no-fee cards, the APR equals the interest rate.

How it is used: The **APR** on Evelyn's credit card was 21.49%, so she was very careful not to carry a balance whenever possible.

authorized user

secondary cardholder

What it is: a person who's named as a holder on someone else's credit card account, giving them full access to using the card

How it works: An authorized user gets added to a credit card account as a secondary cardholder by the primary cardholder. The secondary holder can make purchases and get cash advances as if the card were theirs. Being named as an authorized user can affect your credit score and credit history, as all transactions are reported for both the primary and secondary cardholders. This can help someone build or improve credit as long as the primary shareholder acts in a financially responsible manner (making payments on time every month, for example).

How it is used: Loren added her son as an **authorized user** on her credit card when he went to college.

average daily balance

credit card calculation

What it is: the amount owed on a credit card on each day of the month

How it works: Average daily balance is a calculation created by credit card companies to assess interest charges. Credit card balances can increase and decrease every day, unlike a standard loan that only sees balance changes monthly. The credit card company figures out your balance every day, starting with the prior month's balance due and adding activity day by day for the full billing period. Purchases increase the daily balance, and payments lower it. At the end of the billing period, the company adds up each daily balance and divides the total by the number of days in the billing period to arrive at the average daily balance. Next, it calculates monthly interest charges by multiplying your average daily balance by the daily percentage rate (your annual interest rate divided by 365) and then multiplying that result by the number of days in the billing period.

How it is used: Joanna realized that making small credit card payments throughout the month lowered her **average daily balance** more than making one big payment on the due date.

balance transfer

What it is: refinancing credit card debt by paying off one credit card with another, typically one with a lower interest rate

How it works: A balance transfer is a way to reduce credit card interest costs by moving the total amount due on one credit card onto a different card. This strategy lets you refinance high-rate credit card debt for debt with a temporary 0% (or other extremely low) rate, allowing you to pay down your debt more quickly. This strategy works if you make sure to fully pay off the transferred balance before the temporary low rate expires. However, you must be careful: If you make purchases with a balance transfer card, your payments will go toward them first and not toward your transferred balance. And if the transferred balance isn't paid off in full on time, the card's regular interest rate will kick in retroactively on the remaining portion.

How it is used: Dana used an 18-month, 0% **balance transfer** card to pay off her high-interest credit card debt.

cash advance

What it is: a short-term loan against your credit card, which comes with a different interest rate than regular purchases

How it works: A cash advance gives you instant access to money by allowing you to borrow it directly from your credit card account. Credit card cash advances almost always involve fees, usually between 3% and 5% of the amount borrowed. For example, if you took a $300 cash advance with a 5% fee, your credit card balance would increase by $315. These transactions also come with higher interest rates than normal credit card purchases, running as high as 29.99%.

The card issuer determines how to access the cash. Some cards can be used at ATMs, others require an in-person bank transaction, and others may require the use of credit card convenience checks. The amount you can get per transaction depends on your credit card's cash advance limits and your available credit.

How it is used: Ilona got a **cash advance** because she was $200 short for rent.

credit limit

spending cap

What it is: the maximum you can borrow on a credit card at any given time

How it works: The credit limit on a credit card is the largest balance you can have outstanding. For example, if your credit card has a $1,000 limit and your balance is currently $750, you could charge up to $250 more until you hit the limit. Once you've maxed out a card, you can't use it for spending again until you pay a portion (or all) of the balance. All transactions go toward the limit, including purchases, cash advances, and credit card fees and penalties. Spending more than your credit limit can result in declined charges or over-limit fees.

The card issuer (the lender) determines your credit limit based on your current financial situation and credit history. Credit limits can change as your financial position changes.

How it is used: Rosa was surprised when her credit card company raised her **credit limit** by $500.

grace period

interest-free payment pause

What it is: a time frame during which you can pay off a credit card balance without incurring any interest

How it works: A credit card grace period is between the end of the card's billing cycle (the statement closing date) and the payment due date, usually around 21 days, during which no interest is charged if the balance is paid in full. With this, cardholders can use their cards regularly, pay off the balance, and avoid interest on their purchases. With many credit cards, the grace period applies only to purchases, not cash advances.

If the balance is not paid in full, the grace period won't apply to the outstanding amount or the next billing cycle. Without the grace period, interest charges start from the day of purchase for new charges. Grace periods may be restored after several billing cycles when you pay the balance in full by the payment due date.

How it is used: Angelica wasn't sure if her new credit card had a **grace period**, so she looked at the credit card agreement to find out.

late payment fee
overdue fine

What it is: an amount charged by a credit card company when payment is not made by the due date

How it works: A late payment fee gets charged when you have not made at least the minimum payment due on your credit card balance by the payment due date listed on your statement. These fees are usually fixed amounts (around $30–$40) and must be clearly disclosed in your credit card agreement. Late fees increase your credit card debt, increase your utilization, and affect your credit score.

How it is used: Emma was frustrated by the $32 **late payment fee** on her credit card bill, as her payment was only 1 day late.

minimum monthly payment
least amount of money paid on a credit card

What it is: the smallest payment that can be paid on a credit card balance to keep the card in good standing

How it works: The minimum monthly payment on a credit card is the lowest acceptable payment to keep your account active and avoid late payment fees. It may be a specific dollar amount or a percentage of your balance, depending on how much you owe. Generally, the minimum monthly payment will be the full balance if less than $25, a fixed minimum of $25 to $30 if your balance is less than $1,000, or a percentage of a balance (usually 2%–3%) if more than $1,000. The payment amount is slightly more than the current interest due, and paying the minimum monthly payment will not help you pay your credit card debt. However, paying any amount more than the minimum will help pay down the debt more quickly.

How it is used: Nicole set up automatic **minimum monthly payments** on her credit card account so she never missed one.

over-limit fee

fine for charging too much on a credit card

What it is: a penalty charged by a credit card company when a cardholder's outstanding balance exceeds their credit limit

How it works: Over-limit fees come into play when you spend more than the available credit on your credit card. These fees are uncommon now (due to the CARD Act of 2009) but do exist for cardholders who opt into them instead of agreeing that charges more than the credit limit will be declined. Cards that do come with over-limit fees can't have fees more than the excess charge. So, if you have a $1,000 credit limit and your balance reaches $1,020, the over-limit fee can't exceed $20. In addition, the credit card company can only charge this fee once per billing cycle. Cardholders can opt out of this feature at any time.

How it is used: Nadine was frustrated by the $50 **over-limit fee** on her credit card bill, as she hadn't realized how high her balance was.

penalty APR

higher interest rate

What it is: a high interest rate charged on a credit card balance when 2 months of payments are missed

How it works: Penalty APRs are excessive interest rates, as high as 29.99%, charged when you're 60 days late with your payment. These rates can be applied until you make 6 consecutive months of on-time payments. Penalty APR information must be disclosed by credit card issuers in the credit card terms section with a clearly displayed chart. They must include what triggers the penalty APR, the penalty rate, and how long it can be charged. They must notify you about the rate increase 45 days before it takes effect, so it's often at least 105 days before the penalty APR kicks in. Penalty APRs can be charged on both outstanding balances and new purchases. Not all card issuers use penalty APRs, so you can compare terms online to find one that doesn't.

How it is used: The interest rate on Kaitlyn's credit card nearly doubled when the **penalty APR** started after she missed two payments.

rewards
spending bonuses

What it is: loyalty programs that let cardholders earn gifts based on their credit card spending

How it works: Credit card rewards essentially pay cardholders for using their cards more. Rewards can range from cash, redeemable points for many goods and services, and airline miles. When cardholders in good standing make eligible purchases, they receive rewards. Credit card companies use this as a marketing tool to encourage more spending. Cardholders who pay off their cards every month can actually earn money from their spending through rewards programs. However, people who carry a balance typically pay more in interest and fees than they earn back through rewards.

How it is used: Carrie had credit card **rewards** that gave her 3% cash back whenever she used her card to buy gas.

secured credit card
borrowing attached to a security deposit

What it is: a way to borrow money for everyday spending when you have no or poor credit that also helps you build good credit

How it works: Secured credit cards are designed for people who are trying to establish or repair their credit score. The credit card issuer requires a security deposit (refundable) equal to the card's credit limit as collateral to protect against missed payments. Once the credit card is issued to the cardholder, they use it just like a regular credit card and make monthly payments against the balance. After a period of making consistent on-time payments and more than minimum payments, the cardholder may earn their deposit back.

How it is used: Emmett had poor credit, so he got a **secured credit card** to help repair it.

variable rate

What it is: a credit card interest percentage that changes periodically based on a specific economic index

How it works: A variable rate on a credit card adjusts as economic factors change. The rate is generally tied to a widely used economic index, such as the prime rate (the rate commercial banks offer to their best customers). The variable rate equals the index rate plus a margin (10%–15%) set by the credit card issuer. For example, if the variable rate on your credit card equals "prime plus 12%" and the prime rate is 8.5%, the current rate on your credit card would be 20.5%.

The credit card agreement spells out how often the variable rate could change and is often tied to a change in the index rate. Unlike other rate changes, credit card companies do not have to give 45 days' notice when your variable rate will adjust.

How it is used: Zach had a **variable rate** credit card, and when rates dramatically increased, he carefully paid his whole balance every month.

zero-balance card

What it is: a credit card with no debt balance

How it works: Zero-balance credit cards have no outstanding balance due because either the charges are paid off every month or there's been no spending during the billing period, such as with a credit card that's been paid off and is no longer used, nor is it canceled. Having a zero-balance card can help boost your credit score because it increases your total available credit but not your outstanding balance, effectively decreasing your utilization.

How it is used: Maya rarely used her **zero-balance card** but kept it open to use in case of emergency.

CHAPTER 9

Unsecured Loans: Student Loans and Personal Loans

Many people take out student loans before they fully understand how borrowing money works; they then end up trapped in a seemingly bottomless amount of debt that keeps them from reaching other financial goals. Personal loans can make good financial sense in specific situations but are often used in ways that cause long-term financial problems for people trying to get ahead. With all kinds of unsecured loans, it's crucial to understand every word in the loan agreement because unsecured doesn't mean the lender has no legal rights if the borrower doesn't pay.

This chapter explains the different fees associated with unsecured loans that add to total loan costs. In this chapter, you'll learn about the many kinds of student loans and student loan repayment plans, the financial dangers of payday loans, how to recognize predatory lending tactics, and whether you might qualify for public service loan forgiveness for student loans.

application fee

cost of requesting a loan

What it is: a one-time charge that potential borrowers pay to lenders when asking for a loan

How it works: Application fees are charged by some lenders to cover their costs of processing a loan application and occur with many types of loans. These up-front fees get paid when the borrower applies for the loan, and they're generally nonrefundable even if the loan is denied. Application fees must be fully disclosed to you when you request the loan application. The fees can generally range from $50 to $500, depending on the loan type and amount. Not all lenders have application fees, so borrowers can shop around to find one without extra costs.

How it is used: Lena researched different lenders to find some that didn't charge **application fees**.

direct subsidized loan

federal student loan with interest assistance

What it is: a student loan where the federal government pays the interest while you're still enrolled in school and during your grace period

How it works: Direct subsidized loans are federal student loans for undergrads with financial need. These loans are usually the top choice for college students because they don't need a credit history or a cosigner to be approved. In addition, loan payments aren't required until after graduation, and the federal government pays all interest on the loans as long as the student is enrolled in school at least half-time. This way, unpaid interest doesn't accrue, adding to the loan balance, and the amount due when repayments start will be equal to the amount of money originally borrowed.

How it is used: Fiona got a **direct subsidized loan** to cover her first year of college.

direct unsubsidized loan

federal student loan

What it is: a student loan that gains interest when the funds are provided, even though payments aren't due for years

How it works: Direct unsubsidized loans are federal student loans for undergrads and graduate students. The loan amount is determined by school tuition and other costs of attendance after taking additional financial aid into account. Loan payments aren't required until after graduation, but interest starts accruing the day the funds are given out. The unpaid interest gets added to the balance of the loan, so people who don't make any payments until they leave school will end up owing more than their original loan balance by the time payments are due.

How it is used: Phillip made interest payments on his **direct unsubsidized loans** while he was still in school, so the loan balance didn't increase.

FAFSA (Free Application for Federal Student Aid)

universal loan form

What it is: a form that must be completed by anyone hoping to get assistance from the government to pay for college

How it works: FAFSA is a program used to connect college students with available financial aid based on the school they will be attending and their financial need. It's a one-stop source for the federal government and school administrators, based on application information provided by prospective students and their parents. The potential financial assistance can be any mix of loans, grants, work-study programs, and scholarships. Most families are eligible for at least some level of aid. The FAFSA program determines how much need-based and/or other aid each student qualifies for. You can learn more about FAFSA, including important deadlines for the current school year, by visiting https://studentaid.gov.

How it is used: Shannen completed her **FAFSA** form as early as she could so more grant opportunities would still be available.

graduated repayment plan

student loan with increasing payments

What it is: a federal student loan payment plan that allows for smaller monthly payments in the beginning that increase over time

How it works: The graduated repayment plan is available for federal student loans. It allows for reduced payments initially, which then increase every 2 years, and all payments are made within 10 years. Even the low early payments are designed to cover at least the interest due, which helps prevent negative amortization (an increasing loan balance). This payment plan can work well for people who expect their income to rise steadily over the 10-year period. The graduated payment plan typically does not offer the lowest possible initial payments, as it's designed to fully cover interest and to be paid off completely within 10 years.

How it is used: Holly switched to a **graduated repayment plan** when she got a new job where her salary was expected to increase every year.

IBR (income-based repayment) plan

"what you can afford" loan payments

What it is: a student loan payment plan where monthly payments are recalculated annually to equal 10% of discretionary income

How it works: IBR plans allow people who are struggling with their loan payments to limit their contributions to 10% of their discretionary income (15% for loans issued before July 2014). Here, discretionary income means the difference between your annual adjusted gross income (AGI) and 150% of the poverty guideline of your state based on your family size. On an IBR plan, monthly payments won't exceed the standard repayment amount. You must recertify your income every year and report income changes so appropriate payment adjustments can be made. People applying for IBR plans should be aware that monthly payments may not be enough to cover the interest due, and that can increase the outstanding loan balance, making the loan harder to pay off and increasing the amount of interest paid over the life of the loan.

How it is used: Leo applied online for an **IBR plan** because he didn't make enough money to cover his essential monthly expenses and full student loan payments.

ICR (income-contingent repayment) plan

reduced student loan payments

What it is: a student loan payment plan based on income and family size

How it works: An ICR plan is a student loan repayment plan where monthly payments are recalculated annually to equal the lesser of 20% of discretionary income or what the monthly payments would be if they were calculated over 12 years (instead of 10 years). With this option, the monthly payments may exceed the standard repayment amount. ICR plans were created to help people with lower-paying jobs manage their student loan payments. Loans on ICR plans must be paid back within 25 years. As of July 2024, no new applications for ICR plans are being accepted (except in limited circumstances involving specific consolidated loans).

How it is used: Dean chose the **ICR plan** for his student loans because his teaching salary wasn't high enough to cover standard repayments.

loan servicer

company managing borrower payments

What it is: a government or financial institution that processes all aspects of outstanding loans

How it works: Loan servicers manage loans after the funds have been disbursed. Their main responsibilities include processing loan payments and tracking loan balances. It's common for servicers to change over the life of a loan, and new servicers are supposed to notify people to make any necessary changes to their payments (like setting up autopay, for example).

With student loans, loan servicers also help borrowers stay on top of their loans, switch to different payment plans when necessary, and provide certification for loan forgiveness programs. People with student loan debt can find their servicers (different loans may have different servicers) through the National Student Loan Data System by visiting https://studentaid.gov.

How it is used: Once Annabeth graduated, she began making payments to her student **loan servicer**.

NSLDS (National Student Loan Data System)

federal database of educational financial assistance

What it is: a massive, centralized collection of information relating to student loans and grants

How it works: The NSLDS, run by the US Department of Education, acts as the primary database for federal student aid. It provides users with information such as a summary of their federal student loans, current original and outstanding loan balances, loan history, current enrollment status, and current loan status (such as in default, for example). Authorized users can access their account information by logging in through https://studentaid .gov and navigating to their personal dashboards. The NSLDS does not contain information about private loans.

How it is used: James logged into his **NSLDS** account so he could see all of his federal student loans in one place.

origination fee

cost to get a loan

What it is: a one-time expense that lenders charge to administer and process a new loan

How it works: Origination fees are up-front expenses that lenders charge to cover all the costs associated with issuing a new loan. These fees are commonly charged on personal loans and student loans, and they can range from 1% to 12% of the loan balance. In some cases, the fees are added to the loan balance. In others, the fees get deducted, so the borrower receives less money than they're borrowing. Several factors go into determining origination fees, including the borrower's credit history, employment status, loan amount, and whether there's a cosigner.

How it is used: Josh had to pay a 10% **origination fee** to get a personal loan, so he only received $4,500 cash for the $5,000 loan.

payday loan

What it is: an interest-bearing debt with the next paycheck as collateral

How it works: Payday loans offer fast cash for people who need money before their next paycheck arrives. Though they seem like advances against a paycheck, they typically come with extremely high interest rates, making them harder to pay back. If the loan can't be paid back in full when your paycheck comes in, payday lenders may offer "rollover" loans, basically using a second loan to pay off the first one.

Loan interest on payday loans is often referred to as a fee or finance charge and expressed as dollar amounts rather than interest percentages. For example, the fee may be $15 for each $100 borrowed, which computes to an annual interest of 391% (for a 2-week loan: [[$15 ÷ $100] × [365 ÷ 14]]), more than 18 times higher than the average credit card interest rate.

How it is used: Gloria took a **payday loan** because she couldn't pay her rent.

PAYE (Pay As You Earn) plan

What it is: a federal student loan payment plan based on 10% of discretionary income

How it works: The PAYE plan helps student loan borrowers afford their monthly payments by calculating them as 10% of discretionary income. The payments are based on their home state and family size and can never exceed the amount they would have to pay under the standard payment plan. The payments may not be enough to cover the interest due, which can result in an increasing loan balance. Loans on the PAYE plan are meant to be paid back within 20 years. However, if the borrower made 20 years' worth of payments and still has an outstanding balance, the remaining balance will be forgiven. As of July 2024, no new applications for PAYE plans are being accepted.

How it is used: Mandy made payments every month under her **PAYE plan** but still had a balance due after 20 years.

personal loan

borrowing for general expenses

What it is: unsecured debt not tied to a specific asset purchase

How it works: Personal loans are unsecured, non-revolving debts that can be used for any purpose. Their interest rates tend to be higher than car or home loans but less than average credit card rates. Interest rates on personal loans average 12.35% and are closely tied to the borrower's creditworthiness, so someone with poor credit could end up paying 30% rates or more. Additionally, most personal loans come with fees (like loan origination fees) that increase the cost of borrowing. Personal loans can make good financial sense when they're being used to pay off higher-rate debt (such as payday loans or high-rate credit cards).

How it is used: Katy took out a **personal loan** and used the proceeds to pay off her outstanding payday loans.

PLUS loans

education funding for grad school or parents

What it is: federal student borrowing that can be used by graduate students and parents of undergraduate students

How it works: PLUS loans are federal student loans that help fund costs of higher education that aren't covered by direct subsidized or unsubsidized student loans. These loans can pay for graduate programs, and they can be taken out by parents of enrolled dependent students. They're often referred to as "parent PLUS" or "grad PLUS" depending on the borrower's status. Unlike student loans, PLUS loans require a credit check and can be denied. They also require payments to begin as soon as the loan is disbursed unless the borrower specifically requests a payment deferment period (and interest will accrue during that time). PLUS loans are eligible for certain flexible payment options such as graduated or extended payment plans.

How it is used: Steve and Janet took out parent **PLUS loans** to help fund their daughter's college education.

predatory lending

legal loan sharks

What it is: knowingly taking advantage of desperate or uninformed borrowers

How it works: Predatory lending is the practice of exploiting borrowers by lending the largest loan amount at the highest possible interest rate, regardless of the borrower's ability to pay or their understanding of the loan terms. These lenders often specifically target people in desperate financial situations and who cannot afford the offered loans. The federal government and many states have anti-predatory lending laws, but these lenders use loopholes or simply ignore the law.

Signs of predatory lending include no credit check, blank spaces on contracts ("to be filled in later"), excessively high fees, and false or incomplete disclosures. Predatory lenders will often exert pressure on borrowers to sign before they understand the terms and may use scare tactics to coerce an agreement.

How it is used: Belinda was concerned about **predatory lending** when she saw her loan agreement had several blank spaces and the lender wouldn't answer her questions directly.

PSLF (public service loan forgiveness) program

financial incentive to help the community

What it is: a federal program that offers the opportunity to erase a portion of student loan balances in exchange for work that serves the community

How it works: The PSLF program erases the remaining balance of qualified student loans after certain conditions are met. Those conditions include working full-time for an approved public service employer, such as the government or a not-for-profit organization, and making 120 qualifying monthly loan payments. Only direct federal student loans (subsidized, unsubsidized, and consolidated direct loans) with qualifying payment plans (including income-driven plans) are eligible for loan forgiveness under the PSLF program. If you qualify, you can apply for loan forgiveness using the PSLF Help Tool at https://studentaid.gov.

How it is used: Kyle worked full-time for the public school system and was able to apply for the **PSLF program** as soon as he'd made 120 student loan payments.

repayment term

how long you have to pay off a loan

What it is: the amount of time from receiving loan proceeds and making the final loan payment according to the loan agreement

How it works: The repayment term of a loan, also called maturity, is the period from when funds are disbursed to when the loan is paid. This applies primarily to non-revolving loans, though some revolving loans have maturity dates. The length of the repayment term depends on the type of loan. For example, most mortgages mature in 15 or 30 years, personal loans between 1 and 7 years, and student loans 10 years (on standard repayment plans). Longer repayment terms have smaller monthly payments than shorter maturities (on the same loan), but borrowers pay more interest over the life of the loan. Short loan terms make sense when the borrower can afford higher payments, they want to save money on interest, and the loan is small. Long-term loans work for large loans and borrowers who need manageable monthly payments.

How it is used: The **repayment term** for Steve's car loan was 48 months.

Sallie Mae

private student loan lender

What it is: a corporation that specializes in providing higher-education financing for students and parents

How it works: Sallie Mae is a financial services corporation that focuses mainly on student loans and is one of the largest private education lenders in the country. Originally created as a government entity in the 1970s as an SLMA (student loan marketing association), the company ended its federal ties in 2014 and joined the private sector. Sallie Mae offers education loans to undergrad, graduate, and professional students. While Sallie Mae does offer competitive interest rates on student loans, the company does not offer refinancing and offers repayment terms of only 10 or 15 years.

How it is used: Allison maxed out her federal student loans, so she borrowed the rest of the money she needed from **Sallie Mae**.

SAVE (Saving on a Valuable Education) plan

new income-driven repayment option

What it is: a federal program offering lower loan payments, interest benefits, and potential partial loan forgiveness to people with student loans

How it works: The SAVE plan was launched by the Biden administration in 2023 to protect lower-income student loan borrowers. Like other income-driven repayment plans, it offers reduced monthly payments based on income and family size. The SAVE plan bases payments on a smaller portion of adjusted gross income, has the government cover any interest not covered by the monthly payment, and provides possible loan forgiveness after 10 years for people who borrowed $12,000 or less (though this is being challenged in court as of November 2024).

How it is used: John applied for the **SAVE plan** to lower his monthly student loan payments without having to worry about unpaid interest increasing his loan balance.

student loan

money borrowed for college education

What it is: unsecured debt used to finance higher education, often provided by the federal government

How it works: Student loans provide financial assistance to people who can't afford the full cost of a college education. The federal government is the largest provider of student loans and offers them to all eligible students with financial need enrolling in qualifying schools, regardless of credit history. Students apply for these loans by completing the FAFSA online. The school gets those results and creates a complete financial aid offer, which generally includes federal student loans, for the student. If the student needs additional funds to pay for school, they can apply for private student loans separately.

How it is used: Justin needed to take out **student loans** to pay for college.

Truth in Lending Act

consumer protection law

What it is: a federal law that requires lenders to clearly disclose all costs associated with a loan

How it works: The Truth in Lending Act (TILA) protects any financial borrower by requiring lenders to disclose all critical loan terms before the borrower signs the loan agreement. Those terms include the APR, the length of the loan, and all the fees and charges connected to the loan. The TILA was enacted in 1968 and has been updated several times since. The rules apply to all kinds of lenders and creditors including credit card companies and car loan providers. They help borrowers enter into loans with a clear understanding of the agreement.

How it is used: Thanks to the **Truth in Lending Act**, Erica could compare personal loans on an even playing field to figure out which was best for her.

unsecured loan

borrowing without backup

What it is: money borrowed with no specific collateral attached to it

How it works: Unsecured loans offer money to borrowers for reasons other than specific asset purchases (like houses or cars). These types of loans include student loans, personal loans, and credit cards. Since the loan is not attached to specific collateral that the lender could repossess in cases of nonpayment, interest rates tend to be higher. In addition, these loans have stricter standards for creditworthiness because the borrower's credit history, debt-to-income ratio, and financial situation play a more prominent role in lending decisions.

How it is used: Janetta had several **unsecured loans**, including three student loans and two credit cards.

usury laws

What it is: rules that protect borrowers by capping the interest rates charged on loans

How it works: Usury laws are meant to stop lenders from charging unreasonably high interest rates. These are state laws, and the limits can vary widely depending on where the lender is based. These laws may affect where lenders choose to set up shop, so many states have exempted banks from usury laws to attract their business. Some states set different maximum rates depending on the size and repayment term of the loan. For example, the interest rate on a $10,000 5-year loan that originates in Oklahoma can be up to 36%, Alabama requires the interest rate to "not be unconscionable," and Missouri imposes no limit at all.

How it is used: Gina was shocked to find out that some states allowed lenders to charge more than 100% interest on some loans under their **usury laws**.

CHAPTER 10

Mortgages, Home Loans, and Auto Loans

Home loans are typically the largest secured debts people will ever take on, often followed by auto loans. Because they're backed by collateral, secured loans often (but not always) come with lower interest rates than other types of debt. Secured loans have a wide variety of features, and many of them can be tricky to understand. Since many of these loans are long-term commitments that affect the major assets in your life—homes and cars—it's important to understand how they work or you risk having those assets repossessed.

This chapter will supply the information you need to fully understand the terms of your secured loans, including how different interest types work, what costs can be tacked onto the loans, and how to ensure you understand loan payment calculations before you sign any papers. You'll learn about appraisals, buydowns, escrow, underwriting, and more so you can confidently understand your loan agreements.

5/1 ARM (adjustable-rate mortgage)

5-year fixed then annual adjustment

What it is: a mortgage starting with a 5-year fixed interest rate period followed by annual interest rate changes

How it works: 5/1 ARM loans are adjustable-rate mortgage loans that start with an introductory 5-year fixed-rate period before the annual interest adjustments start. The introductory fixed rates are often lower than a fully fixed-rate mortgage to incentivize borrowers to take on higher-rate loans. Once the fixed period is done, the interest rate becomes adjustable and gets calculated based on an agreed-upon formula. The rates adjust upward if interest rates have risen, which effectively increases monthly payments as well, sometimes significantly. These loans can work well for people who plan to refinance or sell their homes before the 5-year fixed period expires.

How it is used: Rob and Vanessa took out a **5/1 ARM** for their house because they expected to refinance when their credit scores had improved.

ACV (actual cash value) (for cars)

how much a car is worth right now

What it is: the assigned worth of a car based on its current physical condition

How it works: The ACV is the dollar value of a car that's being traded in, repossessed, or purchased. It's calculated by subtracting depreciation from its current market value. The ACV takes many factors into account, including the car's make, model, year, mileage, wear and tear, and overall condition. Generally, it equals how much money you could reasonably sell it for. Car dealers use the ACV as a starting point when negotiating trade-ins and sometimes used car sales.

How it is used: The **ACV** on Gene's car was $5,000, but the dealer only gave him $4,800 in trade-in credit.

adjustable-rate mortgage (ARM) loan

loan with changing interest

What it is: a loan used to buy real estate that charges varying interest over time

How it works: ARM loans come with interest rates that change periodically, usually after a period of low, fixed interest. ARMs may confuse borrowers who focus on the low initial rate without understanding that their payments will increase afterward. With most ARMs, the rates change either every 6 months or every 12 months. The loan's name usually explains the timetable. Therefore, a 3/6 ARM has a 3-year fixed-rate period followed by rate adjustments every 6 months. Adjusted rates are calculated using a predetermined formula based on a common benchmark rate plus a margin (fixed percentage). For example, if the benchmark rate is 6.75% and the margin is 2%, the new adjusted rate would be 8.75%. Rate adjustments may be limited according to the loan contract, placing caps on how much a rate can change each period.

How it is used: Rene and Genevieve got a good deal on a 7/1 **ARM loan** with a low introductory rate when they bought their first house.

appraisal

unbiased valuation

What it is: an independent professional assessment of the value of real estate

How it works: An appraisal is an impartial estimate of some property's value—usually a home that's being bought, sold, refinanced, or borrowed against (such as a home equity loan). Lenders use this information to determine the loan amount, the necessary down payment, and whether the loan will be approved. Usually the lender orders the appraisal, the borrower pays for it, and the results are provided to the borrower as soon as possible, but at least 3 days before closing. If the appraisal seems inaccurate, you can request that the lender reconsider their decision, providing documentation arguing your case.

How it is used: The **appraisal** for the house Liam was buying came in lower than expected.

auto loan

money borrowed to buy a car

What it is: borrowed funds used to finance a car purchase, using the car as assurance

How it works: An auto loan is money borrowed to buy a vehicle where that vehicle acts as collateral for the loan. If the borrower doesn't pay back the loan as scheduled, the lender can repossess the vehicle. Most auto loans are scheduled for 36 to 72 months, which corresponds with how long people usually own vehicles. Though a car dealer may facilitate financing, the lenders are generally banks, credit unions, or other financial institutions. Interest rates on car loans depend on the borrower's credit score, repayment term, loan amount, and type and condition of the vehicle. Lenders may not require down payments for auto loans but will offer better interest rates with down payments of 10% or 20%.

How it is used: Jerrika took out an **auto loan** to buy a car that would get her to work.

base price (auto)

no-frills car cost

What it is: the value of a bare-bones model with no extra features

How it works: The base price of a car, set by the manufacturer, is the cost of that make and model with no extra features included. It's the starting point for the price of any vehicle, and all additional features purchased get added to the price. When you're shopping for a car, you might see this listed as the lowest MSRP (manufacturer's suggested retail price) along with the MSRP for the vehicle with their "recommended" features. Add-ons can include things like a sunroof, seat warmers, and tech packages. The base price does not include any applicable taxes or delivery fees.

How it is used: Carey was excited to find he could afford the **base price** of the car he wanted.

biweekly payment

accelerated loan paydown

What it is: a loan repayment schedule that calls for remittance every other week rather than monthly

How it works: Biweekly payments are part of an accelerated mortgage loan paydown plan where payments are made every other week instead of monthly. This allows for 26 half payments per year, essentially adding in an extra month's worth of payments every year so the loan can be paid off faster. This payment schedule also reduces the total interest, often by tens of thousands of dollars, paid over the life of the loan. Homeowners on a biweekly payment plan also build up home equity more quickly. Many mortgage lenders charge a fee for setting up an official biweekly payment schedule to help offset the lost interest. However, homeowners can make biweekly payments themselves (or make an extra mortgage payment once a year) to achieve similar results.

How it is used: Linnea and Jack made **biweekly payments**, which allowed them to pay off the mortgage 5 years early and save over $34,000 in interest.

buydown

paying to reduce interest

What it is: an up-front payment in exchange for a lower interest rate on a mortgage loan

How it works: Buydowns help potential homebuyers get lower interest rates on their mortgages, at least for the first few years. This process typically involves paying discount points (a one-time prepaid interest fee where one discount point equals 1% of the loan) to the lender. Many motivated sellers and homebuilders use buydowns to help new homeowners more easily afford their initial mortgage payments, though they may increase the home price to cover this cost.

Buydowns can be helpful for people who expect to earn more money in the near future when they'd be able to afford higher mortgage payments. The lower initial interest rate also lowers the mortgage payment during the buydown period, which is usually 2 or 3 years. However, if the homeowner's income doesn't increase, payments after the buydown may be unmanageable.

How it is used: Cecelia got a 7.25% mortgage with a **buydown** that lowered the rate to 5.25% during the first year, reducing her starting mortgage payment by $500.

closing costs

final home-buying expenses

What it is: the total expenses of buying or selling a house that are paid when the deal is finalized

How it works: Closing costs (or settlement costs) are additional expenses related to buying or selling a home. These are settled when the transaction is completed and the home changes hands. Both the buyer and seller may incur separate closing costs. Total closing costs can run between 2.5% and 6% of the purchase price of the home.

Closing costs may include loan origination fees, real estate commissions, property taxes, administrative fees, and private mortgage insurance (PMI). All closing costs must be disclosed to the buyer and seller before the contract settles. Some of the buyer's costs may be negotiable with the lender or paid by the seller as part of the deal.

How it is used: Devin's real estate agent advised them to come up with an additional $8,000 to cover **closing costs**.

deed

ownership record

What it is: a legal document that verifies the owner of a piece of real estate, used to legally transfer ownership

How it works: Deeds are physical documents created by attorneys that prove legal ownership of real estate and allow the transfer of ownership from a seller to a buyer. When a real estate transaction is in progress, buyers (or their representatives) generally conduct title searches to make sure there are no liens (legal claims) on the property. Once the deed is transferred, it gets notarized and filed with the appropriate county with the Recorder of Deeds.

The required information for deeds varies by state but typically includes the names and addresses of the buyer and seller, a description of the property, legal language transferring ownership, details of what the seller received for the property, and the seller's signature.

How it is used: Olivia was excited to get a copy of the **deed** when she closed on her new condo.

down payment

up-front portion of purchase price

What it is: money paid toward an asset purchase to reduce the amount of borrowed funds

How it works: A down payment is a percentage of an asset's price, often a house or vehicle, that's paid up front to reduce the loan needed to cover the full purchase price. The more money you put down, the less money needs to be borrowed. This immediately increases your equity stake in the asset and reduces the interest that will need to be paid. Different lenders require different down payment percentages. For home purchases, FHA loans require at least a 3.5% down payment, many other lenders require at least 10% down, and all home mortgages require the purchase of private mortgage insurance for down payments of less than 20%. Typical down payments for car loans range from 10% to 20%.

How it is used: Bonnie scraped together a 20% **down payment** (with some help from her parents) to buy her condo.

earnest money

good faith deposit

What it is: a payment made to the seller of a house by a potential buyer to indicate their serious intent to purchase the property

How it works: Earnest money is a small percentage (usually 1% or 2%) of the sales price of a house on the market paid by a hopeful buyer to demonstrate their interest in buying the property. In competitive markets, the earnest money can be up to 10% of the sales price. Earnest money is usually held in an escrow account until the closing date, and then the funds are applied to either the down payment or closing costs. Depending on the terms of the agreement, earnest money may be refundable under specific conditions such as substantial problems coming to light during a home inspection.

How it is used: Daisy and Brad paid $15,000 in **earnest money** to get their dream house.

escrow

holding fund

What it is: an arrangement where a third party holds money for two other parties involved in a transaction

How it works: Escrow is a financial agreement that serves as a temporary storage space for assets, often money, necessary for a deal between two parties. The escrow account is held by a neutral third party who accepts, holds, disburses, and releases the assets according to the agreement between the parties. Escrow is often connected with home buying and mortgages. For example, earnest money is typically held in escrow until a home sale is closed. Mortgage lenders often facilitate property tax and homeowners insurance obligations by collecting money from the borrower throughout the year, placing it in escrow, and then paying those bills as they come due.

How it is used: Victoria and Jack chose to let their mortgage company handle insurance and tax bills, so a portion of their monthly mortgage payment went into **escrow.**

FHA (Federal Housing Administration)

government agency overseeing mortgages

What it is: a government program that provides mortgage insurance for lenders and accessible mortgages for lower-income people

How it works: The FHA was created in 1934 to promote homeownership after the Great Depression and serves as part of the Department of Housing and Urban Development (HUD). It's one of very few agencies that's almost entirely self-funded. The FHA offers private mortgage insurance (PMI), which is required for mortgage borrowers with down payments of less than 20% to protect FHA-approved lenders from loss. FHA loans, which all require PMI (even with 20% down payments), are geared toward lower-income homebuyers, first-time homebuyers, and people with poor credit. FHA mortgages require a minimum 3.5% down payment and a credit score of at least 580, though individual lenders may have higher standards.

How it is used: Veronica didn't qualify for a conventional mortgage because of her 600 credit score, but she was able to get an **FHA** loan.

First-time homebuyers (FTHB) programs

assistance for prospective new homeowners

What it is: a way for people to more easily buy their first houses with special loans and loan features

How it works: FTHB programs are offered by most states and nonprofit organizations with federal support. These programs are designed to help people purchase a home if they have not recently or ever owned one. Some of the obstacles this program helps with include loans that require lower down payments and accept lower credit scores, assistance with closing costs, low-interest loans, and even down payment assistance grants. Many FTHB programs offer educational resources to prospective homeowners to help them understand all the work required for homeownership.

How it is used: Fiona and Adam researched **FTHB programs** to get help with their down payment and their loan application.

fixed rate

steady interest percentage

What it is: loan interest percentage that does not change over the life of the loan or for a predetermined period

How it works: Fixed-rate loans come with a single constant interest rate that usually lasts for the entire repayment term but may apply to only a specific period. This allows for predictable and easily budgeted monthly loan payments. Fixed rates are often higher than initial adjustable rates, which can make them seem less appealing.

Fixed-rate loans are more popular when rates are generally low. In a period of rising interest rates, it's beneficial to have a fixed-rate mortgage because the rates won't increase. Additionally, should interest rates decrease dramatically, refinancing to a lower fixed-rate loan can be a financially savvy strategy.

How it is used: Mindy and Brianna got a **fixed-rate** mortgage so they would always know how much their monthly payment would be.

HELOC (home equity line of credit)

revolving loan backed by your house

What it is: a secondary mortgage that lets you tap into the value of your house for cash

How it works: A HELOC allows homeowners to borrow money against their equity stake in their house up to a predetermined limit whenever necessary during a draw period (a specific time frame, such as 10 years). These revolving loans work similarly to credit cards, where you can spend HELOC funds, pay them back plus interest charged at a variable rate, and re-borrow the money at any time without having to take out a new loan until the draw period ends. However, HELOCs are secured by your home, and nonpayment can result in losing your home.

How it is used: Joanna got a **HELOC** to pay for home improvements because the rates were lower than her credit card.

HOA (homeowners association)

group that controls a neighborhood

What it is: a private organization that creates guidelines for and manages a community or subdivision

How it works: HOAs control housing communities by establishing rules, conditions, and restrictions for all their residents. They're supported by mandatory dues paid by all homeowners living in those communities. When you buy a house in an HOA community, you agree to pay their fees and follow their terms. HOA rules are binding, which means they can take legal action against or fine any homeowner who doesn't comply. Common HOA rules include restricting exterior paint colors, fences, yard decorations (like flags and flower beds), and visitor parking. HOAs typically provide common services for their communities, such as snow removal, trash pickup, and swimming pools.

How it is used: Anita was frustrated that her **HOA** wouldn't approve a shed in her backyard.

home equity loan

borrowing against your house

What it is: money borrowed based on the ownership percentage of real estate, usually a primary residence

How it works: Home equity loans are second mortgages that help homeowners tap into the value of their homes without selling the property. They're single-disbursement, fixed-term loans, meaning you borrow a specific amount of money and pay it back within a certain number of years. Home equity loans generally come with fixed interest rates, and because they're secured loans, they tend to have lower interest rates than personal loans or credit cards. When the proceeds of a home equity loan are used to make improvements to the home that will increase its value, the interest payments may be tax deductible for federal income tax purposes.

How it is used: Dale and Bill took out a **home equity loan** so they could put an addition on their house.

homeownership vouchers

financial support for first-time homebuyers

What it is: a program that offers families a way to buy homes and get assistance paying expenses related to homeownership

How it works: Homeownership vouchers are part of the federal HCV (housing choice voucher, also called Section 8) program. Low-income families already in the HCV program can use those vouchers to buy homes and receive financial assistance every month to help cover the costs of owning a home. Homeownership vouchers are available only to first-time homebuyers who meet income requirements and have participated in housing counseling (which helps them understand all the responsibilities and expenses related to owning a home). Local PHAs (public housing authorities) manage these vouchers, and they may not be available in all areas.

How it is used: Liam and Esther were able to buy a townhouse with the help of a **homeownership voucher**.

mortgage

loan to buy real estate

What it is: a loan agreement where money is borrowed to purchase real property, and that property is used as collateral for the loan

How it works: Mortgages are loans to buy real estate that use the purchased property as collateral in case of default. These loans typically come with repayment terms of 15, 20, or 30 years, with 30-year mortgages being the most popular. The interest on them can be either fixed or adjustable, and interest rates on mortgages tend to be lower than rates on most other debt. Mortgages can be used to buy property or to borrow against existing equity in a property.

How it is used: Darrin and Sam took out a 30-year fixed-rate **mortgage** to buy their house.

PMI (private mortgage insurance)

payment guarantee

What it is: protection for lenders offering certain loan terms in the event borrowers don't make full or timely payments

How it works: Private mortgage insurance (PMI) may be required by lenders for borrowers with down payments of less than 20% when they buy a house. This insurance covers the lender in the event the borrower doesn't make payments on their loan. It can help people get mortgages even with smaller down payments, providing protection for the lender. The borrower pays the PMI premiums, usually included with their monthly mortgage payment. Many PMI providers require an up-front premium payment as part of loan-closing costs.

How it is used: Eleanora and Federico had to get **PMI** because they only had a 12% down payment when they bought their house.

prepayment penalty

fee for paying early

What it is: a fee that some lenders charge when borrowers pay off their loans early

How it works: Prepayment penalties are charged by some lenders to discourage borrowers from paying off all or a portion of their loans (usually mortgages) early. The fee compensates the lender for future interest they will lose when a loan is discharged prematurely. The prepayment penalty won't affect small extra payments, like making one extra payment annually, adding $100 to every monthly payment, or even making one lump-sum payment of 10% of the outstanding mortgage. Prepayment penalties usually kick in if the borrower pays off a huge chunk of the loan, more than 20%, usually due to refinancing (very common) or selling the home (less common). If a loan comes with a prepayment penalty, it must be clearly stated in the loan agreement along with an explanation of what triggers it. Prepayment penalties can come to thousands of dollars depending on how they're calculated.

How it is used: Evan's mortgage came with a **prepayment penalty** equal to 6 months' worth of interest if he paid off the loan within the first 5 years.

secured loan

a loan backed by a valuable object

What it is: a loan that uses an object of high value (collateral) to guarantee repayment

How it works: With this kind of loan, the lender will place a claim (called a lien) on the collateral that allows them to take it if the borrower doesn't pay. For example, the lender could repossess a car or foreclose on a house. The collateral doesn't have to have any relation to the loan, though it usually does. For example, a car loan usually comes with a lien on that car. Collateral can be pledged to secure loans not tied to any particular asset (for example, some personal loans may require collateral). Because of the built-in safety net, secured loans (from reputable lenders) typically come with lower interest rates.

How it is used: George pledged his home as collateral when he took on a **secured loan**.

trade-in

What it is: using your old car as a down payment for a new car, reducing the price of the new vehicle

How it works: When you trade in a car, you're using your old car as a partial payment toward the purchase price of a new car. The dealer selling the new car figures out the old car's trade-in value based on a variety of factors such as make and model, year, and condition of the vehicle. This usually results in a lower value than if the car was sold separately, but a trade-in can be more convenient for buyers. If the old vehicle still has an outstanding loan, this may be rolled into the loan for the new car, increasing the total amount borrowed and the total interest paid over the life of the loan.

How it is used: Gina decided to **trade in** her old car rather than trying to sell it herself when she was ready to get a new car.

underwriting

What it is: ensuring a buyer has the means to pay back a loan before it's approved

How it works: Underwriting is a critical part of the loan approval process. During this, the lender will verify your net worth, income, credit history, outstanding debt, down payment sources, and information about the asset you're buying (such as a house or car, if applicable). To do this, you'll be asked to supply information like proof of employment, tax returns, bank statements, and other personal financial documents. Underwriting usually requires loan applicants to complete forms and provide additional information as needed. The process can take a couple of weeks to over a month depending on the lender and how quickly you supply all of the requested information.

How it is used: The **underwriting** department asked Carrie for dozens of documents including 3 years' worth of W-2s and her last two pay stubs.

CHAPTER 11

Dealing with Debt

Any time you borrow money or owe something, you have a debt. Sometimes debt is just a piece of a healthy financial picture, when money has been borrowed and is being paid back on schedule. Other times, though, debt becomes overwhelming, creating a significant financial burden. The latter is the kind of debt this chapter focuses on: problematic debt that needs to be brought under control and how to do that.

Being in debt doesn't mean that you've done something wrong; it just means that you owe more money than you can reasonably manage. As a result, you'll need to figure out a way to make it more manageable. This chapter explains the terms typically associated with troublesome debt such as *arrears*, *default*, and *delinquency*. You'll also find explanations of steps you can take to deal with it, including the differences between the snowball and avalanche methods, forbearance, deferment, and credit counseling. The chapter also includes information about collections, debt consolidation, and bankruptcy. Armed with all this knowledge, you'll be able to begin to form a plan for paying back your debt that works for you.

accrued interest

the owed but unpaid cost of borrowing money

What it is: the percentage calculated on a loan balance that builds up instead of being immediately paid

How it works: Accrued interest on a loan is the percentage fee for that loan that has been incurred but not yet paid. It can happen when an outstanding loan starts charging interest before payments are required, like in the case of most student loans. It can also happen when a full loan payment isn't enough to cover the amount of interest due that month, which can happen with adjustable-rate mortgages and some student loan repayment plans. Any time a monthly loan payment isn't enough to pay that month's interest charge, the interest accrues. Accrued interest may be added to the loan balance and have interest applied to it as well.

How it is used: Accrued interest on Georgia's student loans increased her balance due.

arrears

past-due amount

What it is: money owed that is late being paid back

How it works: Being in arrears refers to missed or late payments on debts or financial obligations (like rent, child support, or utility bills) that put the account into past-due status. Falling behind can include making partial payments or no payments at all. Until the account is brought current, it remains in arrears. Being in arrears may come with consequences such as late fees, reports of nonpayment to credit agencies (which can negatively affect your credit score), eviction (for skipped rent payments), or wage garnishment (depending on the type of obligation). If you have an account in arrears, promptly contacting the person or company you owe money to may help prevent dire consequences.

How it is used: Evelyn's credit score decreased after she was in **arrears** on her personal loan payments.

avalanche method

prioritizing high-rate debt payments

What it is: a debt paydown method that focuses on paying down the highest-interest debt first

How it works: Using the avalanche method to pay down debt involves listing all obligations in the order of their interest rates, from the highest to lowest rate. You make required minimum monthly payments on every debt and put anything extra toward the highest-rate debt until that debt is paid in full. Then the next-highest-rate debt becomes the priority debt, and so on until they are all paid off. The main benefit of the avalanche method is paying less interest overall as debts are being paid off.

How it is used: Danica was using the **avalanche method** to pay off her credit card debt and started with her 24% card.

bankruptcy

debt elimination

What it is: a legal process to relieve some or all of a person's debts when they can't pay those debts back

How it works: Bankruptcy is a legal process where debtors can petition the court to eliminate some or all of their financial obligations. Though it's seen as a monetary "do-over" or clean slate, bankruptcies come with serious consequences that can affect your current and future finances. During bankruptcy cases, the court may order some debts forgiven and some of the debtor's assets liquidated with the proceeds used to pay the creditors a portion of what they're owed. In other cases, the court may create and oversee a manageable debt repayment plan. Once a debt has been discharged in bankruptcy, it's no longer legally enforceable, and creditors cannot continue collection efforts.

How it is used: Clara considered **bankruptcy** when she lost her job and was unable to continue making debt payments.

Chapter 7

liquidation bankruptcy

What it is: a court proceeding where some of a debtor's assets are sold off, and the funds are used to pay creditors

How it works: Chapter 7 bankruptcy eliminates most or all of your debts within 6 months. It requires you to turn over your assets (minus exempt assets) and debts to a trustee of the court. The trustee will usually sell off your assets and use the proceeds to pay your creditors. Exempt assets depend on your state and the value of the assets, but they often include cars, clothing, retirement savings, some of your home equity, and some household furnishings. Under Chapter 7, you may lose your house. After the liquidation and repayment, the remainder of the approved debts get discharged. To start the process, you must fill out extensive paperwork (which requires many personal financial documents) and file a bankruptcy petition plus the filing fee with the court.

How it is used: Debbie was thinking about filing for **Chapter 7** bankruptcy but was worried about which assets would be sold off.

Chapter 13

financial fix-up bankruptcy

What it is: a legal proceeding where creditors get paid back according to an extended court-ordered repayment plan

How it works: Chapter 13 bankruptcy works like a financial makeover, where the court and the debtor come up with an extended repayment plan for debts, usually 3 to 5 years. Under Chapter 13, debts aren't canceled and assets aren't liquidated. The debtor must have stable earned income (from employment or self-employment) to qualify. Payments are based on the debtor's disposable income, meaning any type of income minus necessary living expenses (like groceries and medicine). At the end of the payment period, if the debtor has made all monthly payments, leftover unsecured debts (like credit card debt or personal loans) may be fully discharged.

How it is used: Gina and Rob were having a hard time managing their debt payments, so they filed for **Chapter 13** bankruptcy.

charge-off

What it is: an action taken by a creditor to remove a debt from their books that they don't expect to collect

How it works: A charge-off happens when a creditor writes off a debt that is severely delinquent and not expected to be paid. Though the debt gets removed from the creditor's books, the debtor still legally owes that money. Frequently, lenders sell their charge-offs to debt collectors or other companies that buy debts; whoever purchases the debt can then pursue collections against the debtor.

Charge-offs also get reported to credit agencies. That causes a decrease in the debtor's credit score and a black mark on their credit report. Having a charge-off on your credit can make it hard to borrow money going forward.

How it is used: Geneva didn't make any payments on her store credit card bill for 9 months, and the company recorded a **charge-off**.

collections

What it is: efforts to receive payment for past-due debts

How it works: Debt collections happen when a company (such as a collection agency) attempts to recover unpaid financial obligations. Typically, debt collectors are third parties hired by lenders to get money from debtors, though some large companies may have in-house collections departments. Collections can begin when accounts are at least 30 days past due and may start with late notices. As the debt becomes delinquent, collection activities can get more aggressive, often with frequent phone calls to the debtor or people they know. Collectors can take the debtors to court and sue for the balance due. If the debtor doesn't appear, the collector wins by default and may be able to take money directly from the debtor's bank account, put liens on their property, or even garnish wages.

How it is used: After Dave's account went into **collections**, he started getting phone calls every day from the debt collectors.

credit counseling

What it is: a service for people who have difficulty paying their financial obligations to help them create an effective payment plan

How it works: Credit counseling can help you form a realistic plan to pay back debt and teach you how to only take on debt that you can handle. Credit counselors will determine how much you can pay toward debt every month, convince your creditors to accept the payment terms of your budget, and put a stop to stressful collections calls. It's crucial to make sure you're using a reputable agency because there are a lot of scammers in this space. Most trustworthy credit counseling agencies are set up as nonprofits. They charge very low (sometimes no) fees and have highly trained, certified counselors available to help you. You can find reliable information about credit counseling agencies from the National Foundation for Credit Counseling (www .nfcc.org) or the Financial Counseling Association of America (www.fcaa.org).

How it is used: Frannie and Ed decided to try **credit counseling** because they felt like they were drowning in debt.

debt consolidation

What it is: rolling several outstanding loans into one big loan

How it works: Debt consolidation combines your outstanding debts into one giant debt. If you do this on your own—for example, taking out a lower-interest personal loan and using it to pay off several high-rate credit cards—it can be a smart financial move. Assuming you do this, make all minimum monthly payments on the new debt to avoid potential problems (like penalty rate increases).

Be aware that some debt consolidation companies are scams or looking to make money. Companies promoting debt consolidation may appear like they want to help, but often they're taking advantage of debtors by charging hidden fees, significantly extending the payback period (to collect more interest over time), and increasing interest rates. If you're considering debt consolidation, be wary of any consolidation companies because you could end up in even worse financial shape.

How it is used: Marissa decided to DIY her **debt consolidation** by transferring her three highest credit card balances onto a promotional zero-interest card.

debt settlement

reduction of what you owe

What it is: when outstanding debts get negotiated to have creditors reduce the outstanding balance

How it works: Debt settlement happens when you can't repay the full balance of a debt and ask the creditor to reduce the amount owed (through a charge-off on their side). While this seems like a good idea, it can negatively impact your credit score. Plus, the amount of debt reduction generally counts as taxable income. For example, if you owe $20,000 and negotiate with the creditor to lower that to $12,000, you have to pay taxes on the $8,000 canceled debt amount.

Use caution before hiring a debt settlement company to negotiate for you. This space is full of fraud, and the companies often charge exorbitant up-front fees plus a percentage fee of the canceled debt. You might end up paying out more money than if you hadn't done a debt settlement, so beware.

How it is used: Phil was frustrated to find out that his **debt settlement** deal meant he had to pay more taxes.

default

nonpayment of debt

What it is: when a borrower fails to make the necessary payments on their debt

How it works: Default is an account status used when a borrower doesn't make a specific number (which can vary) of consecutive payments. When a loan or other debt is in default, creditors may go through the courts to recover their money. The consequences differ depending on whether the debt is secured or unsecured. With secured debts, like mortgages and car loans, default can trigger foreclosure (on a home) or repossession of the asset used for collateral. With unsecured debts, the unpaid amount may be charged off, sent to collections, or become the subject of a lawsuit where the creditor may be awarded a direct lien on a bank account or the right to garnish wages. In addition, having a default on your record can lead to a reduced credit score, making it harder to borrow money in the future.

How it is used: After Jonah lost his job, he couldn't pay all his bills, and a few of his credit cards went into **default**.

deferment

debt payment pause

What it is: a temporary postponement or reduction of loan payments authorized by creditors to borrowers having financial difficulty

How it works: Deferment is a tool that people struggling to manage their debt payments can use to temporarily get a break. The borrower must contact the lender (or loan servicer) to request deferment before they stop making payments and must make payments until the deferment is approved. Generally, deferment includes a payment pause or reduction that lasts anywhere from a couple of months to a few years. During the deferment period, interest still accrues on the loan (excluding some student loans) and increases the balance due. The missed payments get tacked onto the loan repayment term. Deferments typically apply to student loans, personal loans, and car loans.

How it is used: Dana and Bobbi contacted their lender to request **deferment** when Dana's diagnosis would keep her out of work for 2 months.

delinquency

past-due debt

What it is: any time a full, on-time debt payment is not made

How it works: Delinquency is a debt status indicating that the borrower has missed one required payment, rendering the debt past due. Delinquency can apply to any type of debt or financial obligation including credit card accounts, taxes, child support, and loans. When a borrower misses multiple payments, their debt status can move from delinquency into default. Missing even a single debt payment can negatively affect the borrower's credit score, as delinquencies are reported to credit agencies. Other consequences of delinquency may include late fees and penalty interest rates being triggered.

How it is used: Bowen's credit card account was in **delinquency** because he forgot to make the minimum monthly payment.

Fair Debt Collection Practices Act (FDCPA)

consumer protection against collectors

What it is: a law designed to protect consumers against aggressive, predatory collectors

How it works: The FDCPA was created to prevent third-party debt collectors from using dishonest or abusive practices when contacting debtors. It puts strict limits on when and how collectors can contact you, how they can speak to you, and who else they can contact (like your friends, family, and employer). For example, debt collectors may not call you after 9:00 p.m. or before 8:00 a.m., publicly communicate on social media about your debt, or contact you at all if they know you're being represented by an attorney. The FDCPA also prohibits harassment like repetitive calls or texts, abusive or obscene language, or threats of any kind. If you believe a collector has violated any part of the law, you can sue them for damages.

How it is used: After the debt collector cursed at Camila and threatened her during their call, she reported them to the Consumer Financial Protection Bureau under the **FDCPA**.

forbearance

loan payment postponement

What it is: a temporary suspension of debt repayment during a period of financial hardship

How it works: Forbearance is a temporary suspension of loan payments, mainly for mortgages and student loans, allowed by the lender when the borrower is unable to make payments. It's an alternative to loan default that could otherwise result in legal action or foreclosure. In most cases, the borrower requests forbearance and must demonstrate the financial need to the lender, then the two negotiate an agreement. This could include a full pause on payments, interest-only payments, or partial interest payments depending on the situation. During the forbearance period, interest still accrues on the loan, and any unpaid interest gets added to the loan balance. Once the forbearance period (usually up to 12 months) expires, the borrower is responsible for making up the missed payments.

How it is used: Marcos and Emilia requested mortgage **forbearance** after he got laid off.

garnishment

forced payments

What it is: a court-mandated order that seizes money from a debtor and pays a third party

How it works: Garnishment allows a third party to directly take money from a debtor and give it to the person they owe. The third party is usually an employer or a financial institution. Garnishment can take the form of redirected wages, bank account seizures, or seized tax refunds to cover the amount owed. This procedure is used in many different circumstances to make sure the various debts get paid, including back taxes, child support, government fines or penalties, and certain types of loans (such as federal student loans).

How it is used: Carolina got a court order for wage **garnishment** when her ex fell more than 6 months behind on child support.

payment plan

financial agreement to manage debt

What it is: an agreement between a borrower and a lender about how borrowed funds will be paid back

How it works: A payment plan is an arrangement between a debtor and a creditor that allows the debtor to pay off what they owe over time. They are often used when a debtor can't pay existing monthly payments or a lump-sum payment, such as a tax bill, and needs to break it up into smaller amounts. While this reduces the required periodic payment amount, it does add more interest to the life of the debt, making it cost more overall.

How it is used: Dwight couldn't pay his entire tax bill in April, so he requested an IRS **payment plan**.

payoff amount
total needed to satisfy a debt

What it is: the amount that needs to be remitted to fully settle an outstanding debt

How it works: The payoff amount shows how much needs to be paid to completely clear a debt on a specific date. It differs from the current balance of the debt because it includes any interest and fees accrued through the intended payment date. You can request a payoff statement for any type of loan, and the lender will provide it with a "good through" date; if the payoff isn't made by that date, the payoff amount won't be valid anymore.

How it is used: Julia was nearing the end of her car loan, so she asked for a **payoff amount** to see if she could be done with it sooner.

phantom debt
nonexistent or noncollectible money owed

What it is: money that collectors try to get even though they can't legally pursue it

How it works: Phantom debt, also called zombie debt, is debt that has already disappeared from your credit report because it's too old to appear or pursue, but a debt collector is trying to revive it. It may also include already paid-off debts or debts that aren't yours, but collectors are aggressively attempting to get you to pay it. You have no legal obligation to pay these debts, including the debts that have passed the statute of limitations. However, if you pay the collector any amount, it can revive the debt and your legal obligation to pay. If a debt collector has contacted you about a phantom debt, you can report them to the FTC (Federal Trade Commission) at www.ftc.gov.

How it is used: Marnie got a call from a debt collector about a **phantom debt** from 10 years ago that she'd already paid, so she reported them to the FTC.

snowball method

prioritizing paying off small balances

What it is: a debt paydown method that focuses on paying down the lowest-balance debt first

How it works: Using the snowball method to pay down debt calls for listing all obligations in the order of their balance due from the smallest to the largest. You make the required minimum monthly payments on every debt and put anything extra toward the lowest-balance debt until that debt is paid in full. Then the next-smallest-balance debt becomes the priority debt, until they are all paid off. The idea is that knocking out small debts first helps you gain momentum—snowballing—to pay off larger debts.

How it is used: Ashley used the **snowball method** to pay off her smaller debts, making it easier to manage the larger ones.

validation notice

full information about a debt

What it is: a document that debt collectors are required to provide listing the details of a financial obligation

How it works: A validation notice (also called validation letter or verification of debt) must be supplied by debt collectors within 5 days of the first contact. Requesting the validation notice is the first step any person getting collection calls should take to verify the legitimacy of the claim. The notice must include full details of the debt, complete contact information for the collections company, and a clear explanation of how the debt can be challenged. If the debt doesn't match your records perfectly (for example, it says you owe $79.97, but you actually owe $79.79) or isn't yours, you can dispute it immediately.

How it is used: Delia requested a **validation notice** after she got a collections call for an unrecognized debt.

CHAPTER 12

Investing Terms

Investing can help you build wealth when you understand all the complexities, risks, and rewards. It's not the same as saving, though that's a common misconception, because you can lose the money you invest. When you come to investing with understanding, information, and a plan, you will have the best chance to grow your money. The biggest risk to investors is jumping in without knowing exactly how investing works, which can lead to emotional decisions. You can avoid that fate by building up your knowledge and making intentional investing choices.

This chapter will give you a look inside the big exchanges (NYSE and Nasdaq), critical investment benchmarks like the Dow and the S&P 500, and the important difference between investing and trading. You'll learn about the most common investments like stocks and bonds, how to determine your risk tolerance, and exactly how you can make money by investing (such as capital gains and compounding).

accredited investor

special access

What it is: a wealthy individual qualified to buy securities not available to the public

How it works: An accredited investor is a person with special access to investments that are not accessible to the public, giving the investor expanded investment opportunities. To qualify as an accredited investor, the person must have a net worth of at least $1 million (not including their primary house), income over $200,000 annually ($300,000 if combined with spouse) for at least the past 2 years, and a realistic expectation that the income level will be maintained. It also requires a level of financial sophistication, as these securities are investments in early-stage companies not registered with the Securities and Exchange Commission (SEC).

How it is used: Juana aspired to become an **accredited investor** so she could get in on ground-floor investment opportunities.

asset classes

different types of investments

What it is: groups of securities that work the same way and perform under the same legal guidelines

How it works: Asset classes are baskets for grouping similar types of securities. The major asset classes include stocks, bonds, real estate, and cash. Other asset classes include things like commodities (such as oil and soybeans), cryptocurrencies, financial derivatives (like stock options), and currencies (like euros and dollars). Different asset classes tend to perform differently under the same economic conditions, which can help balance portfolio risk and protect investors against some losses.

How it is used: Mia made sure she had a good mix of **asset classes** in her investment portfolio.

benchmark

What it is: a standard, typically a widely known index, used to measure investment performance

How it works: A benchmark is a set of standards used to compare and evaluate how well (or poorly) investments are performing. Common investment benchmarks include the S&P 500 for stocks and stock-based funds and US treasuries for bonds. These benchmarks represent specific asset classes or subsets of those asset classes as a common measure. You can use them to analyze different investments you're considering or to see how well your portfolio (or portions of your portfolio) fares.

How it is used: Jane compared her portfolio performance to a **benchmark** to see how it was keeping pace.

bond

a loan to a business or government

What it is: a way for companies and government entities to raise funds through borrowing

How it works: Bonds provide a way for businesses and governments to raise capital by borrowing money. When you buy a bond, you're lending money to the issuer (the entity funded by the loan) in exchange for repayment plus interest. Unlike other loans, bonds tend to pay interest periodically (such as quarterly or semiannually) and then repay the principal in one lump sum at maturity. Bonds are considered fixed-income securities, meaning you know exactly how much interest you're going to receive on schedule while you hold them.

How it is used: Rafael included some **bonds** in his portfolio on the recommendation of his financial advisor.

capital gains (or losses)

result of selling an investment

What it is: the amount of money earned (or lost) when a security is sold

How it works: Capital gains occur when assets, such as investments, are sold for more money than you paid for them. If you sell them for less than you paid, then you'd have a capital loss. Capital gains/losses apply to all types of assets, including stocks, bonds, real estate, and cryptocurrencies. Your capital gain is calculated by subtracting the full cost (the basis) of an asset from its selling price. For example, if you bought 100 shares of stock for $10 each, then were charged $10 in fees, your basis would be $1,010. If you then sold those shares for $1,200, you would have a capital gain of $190.

How it is used: Charles made a profit on his first stock sale, earning $200 in **capital gains**.

commodities

basic goods

What it is: raw materials that can be used as is or transformed into other products

How it works: Commodities are the basic materials that can be used for final products or, sometimes, consumed directly, though they're not sold directly to consumers. Commodities include metals (like copper, silver, aluminum, gold, and platinum) and also include other types of raw materials (like soybeans, cocoa, sugar, crude oil, coal, and cattle). Commodities are interchangeable (fungible) goods, meaning it doesn't matter which barrel of oil or bag of coffee is traded because they're all the same. Adding commodities to a portfolio can help reduce the overall risk with another asset class. Investors can purchase commodities options and futures as investments rather than purchasing the goods themselves. These types of investments are sold on specialized commodities markets.

How it is used: Darien bought a **commodities** mutual fund to diversify his portfolio.

compounding

earnings generating more earnings

What it is: when investment earnings produce their own additional earnings

How it works: Compounding occurs when an investment generates earnings, and then those earnings also produce earnings, allowing the original investment to grow faster. This financial power helps you build wealth with less effort, as your investment does the work for you. This process only works if you reinvest your earnings, meaning you buy additional investments with your earnings rather than cashing them out. For example, if you own a stock that earns dividends, reinvesting those dividends in additional shares would lead to those new shares earning future dividends. Overall, the earnings base for your investment would grow over time, producing additional income and potential capital gains.

How it is used: Thanks to the power of **compounding** for 10 years, Ernie's retirement account grew to $31,600 even though he only contributed $24,000.

cost basis

full purchase price

What it is: the total amount paid for an asset, such as a security, including fees, commissions, and other expenses

How it works: The cost basis of an investment includes the amount paid for it plus any additional transaction expenses (like brokerage fees). It can also include reinvested dividends (for stocks) and reinvested capital gains (for funds). The cost basis amount matters because it's used to determine eventual capital gains (or losses) and can affect the amount of taxes due when an asset is sold. It's critical to track the cost basis of investments so you don't end up miscalculating gains or losses or overpaying taxes.

How it is used: Lee kept all her annual brokerage statements so she could keep track of the **cost basis** of each of her investments.

the Dow (DJIA)

stock market benchmark

What it is: a widely reported index used to track the performance of the US stock market

How it works: The Dow, formally known as the Dow Jones Industrial Average (DJIA), is one of the most widely recognized indicators of American stock market performance and trends. The Dow follows the stocks of 30 of the largest and most influential US corporations, all actively traded on either the NYSE or the Nasdaq. When this index is discussed in the news, movement is referred to in points rather than dollars (1 point doesn't equal $1) because the Dow is a price-weighted index. Despite its full name, many of the corporations included in the Dow aren't technically industrial companies; some member companies include American Express, Apple, and UnitedHealth Group.

How it is used: Roni's dad always got excited when **the Dow** reached new highs and checked his portfolio whenever the index dipped more than 50 points.

ESG (environmental, social, and governance) investing

using nonfinancial factors to select securities

What it is: prioritizing socially responsible, ethical companies when choosing assets for your portfolio

How it works: ESG investing (also called impact investing or sustainable investing) involves looking at corporate actions before choosing investments rather than just looking at the financial picture. Companies are judged on their treatment of issues like the environment, gender equality, fair pay, policies, and hiring diversity. These factors are considered along with standard financial metrics like earnings, growth, and share prices. Companies that fall short are screened out; this may include companies that produce toxic waste, treat animals inhumanely, prioritize CEO pay over employees, or have unsafe workspaces.

How it is used: Debbie was passionate about green living and focused on **ESG investing** in her portfolio.

index

widely used benchmark

What it is: a constructed measurement of a specific set of securities chosen to represent a portion of a securities market

How it works: An index follows the performance of a predetermined basket of securities. Investors can use indexes to evaluate the performance of their portfolios and individual investments. Indexes can track an entire market (like the stock market or bond market) or a subset of it (such as tech companies or high-risk corporate bonds). Many investors and fund managers aim to "beat the market" by outperforming relevant indexes, a strategy that rarely works consistently over the long term. Commonly used indexes for investing include the S&P 500, the Dow Jones Industrial Average, and the Nasdaq Composite.

How it is used: Iris measured her retirement portfolio performance by comparing it to an appropriate **index**.

Nasdaq

large stock exchange

What it is: an American-based electronic marketplace for buying and selling securities

How it works: The Nasdaq is the world's second-largest stock exchange. Originally called NASDAQ (National Association of Securities Dealers Automated Quotations), the exchange was launched in 1971. It became the first electronic stock market in the world and the first to offer online trading. With its tech-based foundation, the Nasdaq attracted many leading tech and biotech companies. This exchange now includes 29 markets in North America and Europe, providing a global marketplace for securities with more than 5,000 companies listed and available to trade worldwide.

How it is used: Ron likes to follow the **Nasdaq** to see the performance of his favorite tech companies.

NYSE (New York Stock Exchange)

main place to trade shares

What it is: the oldest and largest platform for buying and selling securities in the US

How it works: The NYSE is the world's largest and most utilized stock exchange. It holds more than 25% of the total global equities market, with more than \$28.8 trillion in total market capitalization listed. The NYSE serves two main purposes: giving companies a space to list their shares and giving investors a marketplace to buy and sell those shares. It uses an auction-style system where sellers try to auction shares for the highest prices and buyers submit bids for those shares. The NYSE has strict listing requirements for public companies, such as they must have at least 1.1 million publicly traded shares with a minimum share price of \$4. The companies must also demonstrate profitability with earnings of \$10 million or more over the prior 3 years.

How it is used: Americans have been investing in stocks over the **NYSE** since 1792.

portfolio

basket of investments

What it is: a collection of securities designed to work together according to your financial goals

How it works: A portfolio is a group of different investments owned by a single person or entity. The combination of securities differs based on the unique goals, timeline, and risk tolerance of the owner. You can have more than one sub-portfolio; for example, one might hold retirement account investments and another might hold non-retirement investments, but together they make up your total portfolio. The most common portfolio holdings include stocks, bonds, cash, and real estate, though some of those may be held as mutual funds or exchange-traded funds.

How it is used: Ally went to a personal financial planner to help her design her optimal investment **portfolio.**

returns

investment earnings

What it is: the amount of money produced by investments, including regular earnings (like dividends) and investment growth

How it works: Returns on investments refer to the amount of money you earn by holding or selling them. Different types of investments offer different kinds of returns. For example, stocks may provide dividends, bonds provide interest, and funds may provide a combination of those plus capital gains distributions. All investments generate capital gains (or losses) when they're eventually sold. The total return on an investment includes all the earnings produced while it's held plus gain (or loss) when it's sold or redeemed.

How it is used: Eli's portfolio generated **returns** of 10% last year.

risk/reward ratio

balance between loss and gain potential

What it is: a measurement of expected return compared to possible loss

How it works: The risk/reward ratio (sometimes called risk/return ratio) helps investors evaluate whether the potential returns on an investment are worth the potential loss. This ratio can be used to compare different investment options or analyze single investments. The lower the value of the ratio, the less risk per unit of gain, meaning the potential for reward outweighs the downside risk. The risk/reward ratio is calculated by dividing the potential loss (usually the amount invested) by the potential gain (expected returns). For example, investing $1 hoping to double it to $2 gives you a risk/reward ratio of 1:2, willing to risk $1 for a reward of $2.

How it is used: Stefania looked at **risk/reward ratios** when she was comparing different securities to invest in.

risk tolerance

fear of loss

What it is: the level of comfort in withstanding temporary investment losses in search of potential future gains

How it works: Risk tolerance refers to the amount of risk an investor is willing to take on (and potentially sustain if they lose) in the pursuit of profits, as investment values can be volatile. Understanding your risk tolerance can help you make better investment choices that are more suitable. Your risk tolerance may change over time depending on factors like your age, family size, current financial situation, and earnings prospects. People with high-risk tolerances tend to be more aggressive investors, putting their money into securities with high-profit potential and relatively big downside risk. People with low-risk tolerances focus more on preservation and stability than growth potential.

How it is used: As Dean got older, his **risk tolerance** decreased, and he started shifting more of his portfolio away from aggressive investments.

S&P 500 (Standard & Poor's 500)

stock market index

What it is: a benchmark that tracks the 500 largest companies traded on the US stock market

How it works: The S&P 500 is a major stock-tracking index that includes 500 of the largest and most influential corporations, weighted by their market capitalization (the value of their outstanding shares). To qualify for inclusion, the companies must be US-based trading on a US exchange, have a market cap of at least $15.8 billion, and show positive earnings for the most recent five quarters. Some companies in the index include Microsoft, Amazon, and ExxonMobil.

The S&P 500 index is used to judge the overall performance of the US stock market. Many funds track the composition of the index, allowing investors to partake indirectly in its performance.

How it is used: Trent followed the ups and downs of the stock market by tracking the **S&P 500**.

stock

piece of a company

What it is: a security that represents an ownership share in a corporation

How it works: A stock is a piece of a corporation, and someone with stock has an ownership stake in that corporation. Companies issue stock to raise money to fund their operations. In exchange, stockholders own their proportional share of the company and are entitled to that portion of the company's earnings and assets. Stocks are originally sold directly by the company through an initial public offering (IPO). After that, stock shares trade on the secondary market, not involving the corporation itself. Investing in stocks offers potential financial growth through both income production and capital gains. Investors buy and sell shares through brokers over stock exchanges.

How it is used: Gail was interested in buying **stocks** to build up her net worth.

trading

constant buying and selling

What it is: frequent buying and selling of securities to profit from relatively small price changes

How it works: Trading is a strategy where people buy and sell securities frequently to cash in on rising or falling stock prices as they occur. The focus is on short-term gains due to market volatility. Traders often specialize in certain types of securities such as stocks, commodities, currencies, or derivatives. They aim to outperform traditional buy-and-hold investing strategies using a technical analysis of market movements to capitalize on momentary price shifts. Traders tend to take on more risk than investors and dedicate a great deal of time to their practice.

How it is used: Evan tried his hand at **trading** but couldn't tolerate all the daily ups and downs.

CHAPTER 13

Stocks and Bonds

Stocks and bonds are the most commonly traded securities, and most people's investment portfolios contain both. Though they work in very different ways, both stocks and bonds can help people build wealth and generate income. By tapping into the strengths of each, investors can better balance risk and rewards for a more stable portfolio.

In this chapter, you'll get a more in-depth look at the different types of stocks and bonds, from blue chips and preferred stock to Treasury bills and junk bonds. You'll learn about interest and dividends, market capitalization, the differences between government and corporate bonds, and how to determine yield. This chapter will help give you a more solid understanding of the inner workings of debt (bonds) and equity (stocks) securities so you can invest with confidence and achieve your financial goals.

blue chip

What it is: publicly traded stock with a long-established positive track record

How it works: Blue chips are considered to be the most prestigious, well-established publicly traded companies. Most of them have existed for decades and have remained leaders in their respective industries; they are companies everyone knows. Blue chips are financially sound, solid performers with proven track records, making them good choices for more conservative and buy-and-hold investors. The main appeal of blue chips is consistency in both earnings and growth, along with a reliable history of paying out dividends. Examples of blue chips include IBM, Walmart, and Home Depot.

How it is used: Martha and Ben held several **blue chips** for decades, sold them, and used the proceeds to fund their retirement.

bond discount

What it is: the excess of face value over market price

How it works: A bond discount is the difference between the bond's face value and its current market price, where it can be bought for less than the amount due when the bond matures. For example, if you buy a $1,000 bond (its face value) for $975, the bond was sold for a $25 discount. Bonds are typically sold at a discount when interest rates have increased and the rate paid by the bond is lower than prevailing rates. When a bond is issued at a discount, it has a built-in gain equal to the amount of the discount because the bond will eventually be redeemed for its full face value (even though you've bought it for less) and interest will be paid based on the face value.

How it is used: Brody took advantage of a **bond discount** to add some fixed income securities to his portfolio.

bond premium

higher-priced bond

What it is: the excess of market price over face value

How it works: A bond premium is the difference between the bond's face value and its current market price, where its current price is more than the amount due when the bond matures. For example, if you buy a $1,000 bond for $1,050, the bond was sold for a $50 premium. Bonds are typically sold at a premium when interest rates have decreased and the rate paid by the bond is higher than prevailing rates. That means the bondholder will get more in interest income from the bond than they could with another investment at the current market rate.

How it is used: Marina paid a **bond premium** because she expected interest rates to drop even further and wanted to lock in some predictable income at a higher rate.

common stock

shares in a corporation

What it is: basic equity securities representing corporate ownership

How it works: Common stocks are bare-bones securities that represent ownership stakes in a corporation. These are the most widely owned types of stocks for the general public, and they're heavily traded over the stock exchanges. Shares of common stock provide voting rights and a claim on the proportional share of corporate assets and income, though common stockholders are last in line in the event of liquidation. Common stockholders are entitled to receive dividends only when they are declared and distributed by the corporation, usually paid out of corporate earnings.

How it is used: Arturo's retirement portfolio held mostly **common stock**.

corporate bond

company borrowing from the public

What it is: debt issued by a corporation to raise money

How it works: Corporate bonds are issued by corporations as a means of borrowing money. In exchange for the loan, bondholders receive periodic interest payments and a promise that the face value of the bond will be repaid on or before a specific maturity date. Corporate bonds are evaluated by rating agencies to determine their likelihood of being repaid. This helps investors determine the risk level involved in a corporate bond purchase. These bonds are considered fixed-income securities that provide regular, reliable interest payments.

How it is used: Candi had some **corporate bonds** in her portfolio to earn consistent interest.

dividend

payments to shareholders

What it is: a portion of corporate earnings periodically paid out to shareholders

How it works: A dividend is a proportional share of a corporation's profits that gets paid out to its stockholders. The amount is decided by the corporation's board of directors, usually based on current earnings, and the dividends are typically paid out quarterly. Those dividends can be paid out in money or in additional shares of stock (called stock dividends). Corporations are not required to pay dividends, and many don't, keeping the money instead to reinvest into the company's operations.

How it is used: Anita earned enough in **dividends** from her investments to help her pay some bills.

I-bond

federal obligation with inflation protection

What it is: US Treasury savings bonds with interest rates that adjust to inflation

How it works: I-bonds (or Series I bonds) are US Treasury debt obligations available for purchase to the general public. To offer some inflation protection, the interest rate on I-bonds changes every 6 months either up or down based on inflation. I-bonds have 30-year maturities and compound interest every 6 months. The full interest earned is paid out when the bond matures. If you cash in an I-bond before its maturity (allowed any time after the first year), you forfeit the last 3 months of interest. I-bonds can be purchased from the Treasury directly at https://treasurydirect.gov.

How it is used: Ruby decided to buy **I-bonds** as long-term investments for their security and inflation protection.

junk bond

high-risk corporate debt

What it is: a high-interest, high-risk debt security issued by a corporation with questionable creditworthiness

How it works: Junk bonds are debt securities with low credit ratings, indicating a high potential for default. To raise money, corporations with shaky finances issue these bonds and offer better interest rates (often up to 6% higher) than companies with solid credit. Investors with a high risk tolerance and the ability to absorb losses may choose junk bonds for their significantly higher returns. Many junk bond issuers are unable to make their scheduled interest payments or redeem the bond on its maturity.

How it is used: Gavin took a gamble with **junk bonds**, hoping to capitalize on their high interest rates.

large cap

biggest corporations by market share

What it is: companies with a market capitalization of over $10 billion

How it works: Large cap, or large market capitalization, refers to corporations (and their stock) with more than $10 billion of market value. These tend to be well-established, historically profitable corporations like Apple, Amazon, and Alphabet that make up the lion's share of the total US stock market. They are often included in leading indexes like the S&P 500 and the Dow. Large-cap stocks can add stability and income to a portfolio, providing steady (but slower) long-term growth and often regular dividends.

How it is used: Kenneth and Yolanda included a **large-cap** stock fund in their investment portfolio.

market capitalization

value of corporate stock

What it is: a measurement of a corporation's value based on its outstanding traded stock shares

How it works: Market capitalization (also called market cap) is a calculated value describing a corporation's worth in terms of its stock market presence. It is equal to the total number of shares outstanding multiplied by the current per-share stock price. For example, if a corporation has 30 million shares outstanding and its market price is $50 per share, the market cap would be $1.5 billion. Market cap is not a direct measure of the corporation's net worth or earnings; it only reflects the value of the company on the stock market. It helps investors quickly assess what the market thinks a company is worth.

How it is used: Tatiana included **market capitalization** as a factor when comparing different stocks to buy.

micro cap

very small corporations by market share

What it is: companies with market capitalization between $50 million and $300 million

How it works: Micro cap refers to corporations with $50 million to $300 million of stock market value. These tend to be more volatile, risky stocks of unproven corporations, and they're harder to trade due to lower market demand. Information about micro-cap stocks can be limited and hard to find, adding more risk to the investment because this space is full of stock scams (like fake companies). Micro caps don't trade over the major exchanges like the NYSE; they trade in the OTC (over-the-counter) market. They introduce higher risk in a portfolio but also more potential for big gains if the company takes off.

How it is used: Milo invested in **micro caps** in the hopes that he was buying early into the next Apple or Amazon.

mid cap

What it is: companies with market capitalization between $2 billion and $10 billion

How it works: Mid cap refers to corporations with between $2 billion and $10 billion of market value. These companies can provide a good balance between stability (more than small cap, less than large cap) and growth potential (less than small cap, more than large cap). Investors expect that these companies will, over time, grow more and increase their profits and sales, possibly eventually moving over into the large-cap bucket. Mid-cap companies won't be as familiar as large caps and include companies (as of 2024) such as Duolingo, AbbVie, and Texas Roadhouse.

How it is used: Harry and Ian decided to keep at least 20% of their investment portfolio in **mid-cap** stocks for their growth potential.

municipal bonds

What it is: debt securities issued by state and smaller government entities to fund public works projects

How it works: Municipal bonds (also called munis) are debt securities used by states, cities, and localities to raise money for operations and special projects. In exchange for the loan, the bondholder receives regular (usually semiannual) interest payments and gets repaid the full face value of the bond at its maturity. Municipal bond interest is not subject to federal income taxes and is often not taxable at the state or local level if you live there. This effectively increases municipal bonds' yield compared to other bonds (like corporate bonds) whose interest is subject to full taxation.

How it is used: As Randy got older, he moved a bigger portion of investments into safe, tax-friendly **municipal bonds**, which helped fund a new park in his neighborhood.

par value

face value

What it is: the issuance value of a bond or stock as indicated on its certificate

How it works: Par value, also called face value, is the assigned value of a stock or bond when it's issued. For bonds, the par value is the amount of principal that will be paid to the bondholder at its maturity. Typically, par value for a bond is set at $100 or $1,000, with $1,000 being more common.

For stocks, par value is usually a minimal number chosen to comply with state law that forbids stocks to be sold for a price below their par value, though not all states have this rule. It's usually set very low, close to zero, to protect shareholders if the corporation can't pay all of its debts. With both stocks and bonds, par value generally has little or no effect on the security's market value.

How it is used: Albert bought five bonds with $1,000 **par value** each and would collect $5,000 when they matured.

preferred stock

shares with favored treatment

What it is: corporate shares that receive prioritized promised dividends

How it works: Preferred stocks act like a combination of stocks and bonds. Like common stock, they represent ownership shares of a corporation. Like bonds, they generally come with redemption dates and promised fixed dividends that are paid out regularly, regardless of the company's earnings. Preferred stocks don't come with voting rights, they don't experience the same market price growth as common stocks, and they usually don't get to participate in earnings even when the company has a very successful year. Preferred dividends get paid out before common stock dividends.

How it is used: Barry held some **preferred stock** in his portfolio to increase his dividend income.

Series EE bond

nonmarketable Treasury debt security

What it is: a hybrid debt/savings vehicle issued by the US Treasury

How it works: Series EE bonds are Treasury-issued savings bonds guaranteed to double in value in 20 years. These bonds will pay out interest for up to 30 years (their maturity), unless they're cashed out earlier. The minimum investment allowed for Series EE bonds is $25, but you can buy any amount more than that up to $10,000 per year. These nonmarketable (meaning they aren't sold on the open market) bonds can't be redeemed for the first year, and any redemption within the first 5 years forfeits 3 months of interest. The longer Series EE bonds are held, the more interest they accumulate, increasing the redemption value. You can buy Series EE bonds at https://treasurydirect.gov.

How it is used: Will and Tina bought **Series EE bonds** when their child was born so they'd have a small nest egg by the time they turned 20.

shares

pieces of a corporation

What it is: units of company ownership

How it works: Shares are ownership units in a business, usually a corporation whose shares are called stocks. Investors buy these units, paying for a stake in ownership of the company. The corporation's formation documents specify the maximum number of shares allowed, called authorized shares. Then the board of directors decides how many of those authorized shares to issue, meaning to be sold to investors; not all authorized shares get issued. Shares can be privately held or publicly traded, and publicly traded shares are bought and sold over public stock exchanges after their initial public offering (IPO).

How it is used: Felicia bought **shares** in a dozen corporations she was familiar with.

small cap

What it is: companies with market capitalization between $300 million and $2 billion

How it works: Small cap refers to corporations with between $300 million and $2 billion of market value. These tend to be younger, less-established corporations that hope to eventually grow into large caps in the future. Because they're not yet established, these companies tend to be riskier investments than large and mid caps, but they have more growth potential. Their shares are typically more affordable, largely because institutional investors (like mutual funds) can't invest heavily in small caps (by regulation), which helps keep their prices lower. It can be difficult to find full information on small caps, and they are harder to sell when you're ready due to lower trading volume.

How it is used: Jeremy did a lot of research and chose several **small-cap** stocks for his portfolio to increase its growth potential.

Treasury bill

What it is: a US government debt security with a maturity of 52 weeks or less

How it works: Treasury bills (called T-bills) are short-term federal debt obligations that mature within 1 year (between 4 and 52 weeks) and are backed by the full faith and credit of the US government. They are normally issued at a discount (though they may be issued at par value) and sold in increments of $100 (with the maximum being $10 million). Interest is paid in full when the T-bill matures and equals the difference between the purchase price and par value. That interest is subject to federal taxes but exempt from state and local taxes. T-bills can be purchased directly from the US Treasury (at https://treasurydirect.gov) or on the secondary market.

How it is used: Fred decided on **Treasury bills** as a place to put some savings because they earned more interest than a regular savings account.

Treasury bond

long-term US government debt

What it is: a US government debt security with a maturity of 20 or 30 years

How it works: Treasury bonds (or T-bonds) are long-term federal debt obligations that mature in either 20 or 30 years. They pay out interest semi-annually based on the stated coupon (interest) rate and the full par value at maturity. Interest on Treasury bonds is taxable on the federal level and tax-exempt on the state and local level. These bonds are considered risk-free because they are backed by the full faith and credit of the US government.

How it is used: Bernadette included some **Treasury bonds** in her portfolio to help balance out its risk profile.

Treasury note

medium-term US government debt

What it is: fixed-rate government debt security with a maturity between 2 and 10 years

How it works: Treasury notes are fixed-rate debt securities issued by the US government and pay out interest semiannually. They are issued with maturities of 2, 3, 5, 7, or 10 years, and the full face value of the note is paid back at maturity. Treasury notes can be bought from https://treasurydirect.gov or on the secondary market. These investments offer a risk-free and pre-dictable income stream, making them a good choice for risk-averse investors or as a balance for an otherwise high-risk portfolio.

How it is used: Pauline inherited some **Treasury notes** from her grand-mother and decided to keep them to lower the overall risk in her portfolio and get the semiannual interest payouts.

yield

earnings on a security

What it is: the total income earned on a security, generally expressed as a percentage

How it works: Yield represents the returns on an investment. For stocks, that includes dividends; for bonds, that includes interest. For any type of investment, yield includes price increases (capital gains). Yield is calculated by dividing the total returns on an investment by its purchase price. For example, if you bought 100 shares of stock for $200 and received $20 in dividends, the yield would be 10% ($20/$200). Yield can be calculated using different factors, such as before-tax or after-tax earnings.

How it is used: Deidre was excited when her total portfolio **yield** topped 10% for the year.

CHAPTER 14

Mutual Funds, Exchange-Traded Funds (ETFs), and Real Estate Investment Trusts (REITs)

Mutual funds, exchange-traded funds (ETFs), and real estate investment trusts (REITs) have one big thing in common: They all offer shares in baskets of underlying securities, allowing investors to achieve diversification with a relatively small investment. They're great choices for novice investors beginning to build portfolios and solid additions for investors looking to broaden their holdings. Funds tend to offer the same income and growth potential as the assets they hold; for example, stock funds may offer dividend payouts and capital appreciation, just like individual stocks would.

In this chapter, you'll learn how funds can reduce portfolio risk, increase asset allocation and diversity, and make investing easier overall. You'll find out more about the different costs and fees involved with fund investing, the importance of net asset value, what REITs are, and how index funds work. You'll gain insights into the differences between mutual funds and ETFs and between property REITs and mortgage REITs. Plus, you can more easily figure out how funds fit into your portfolio and help advance your financial goals.

asset management

choosing and handling fund investments

What it is: the practice of making investments and trades for funds, attempting to increase their value

How it works: Asset management (or portfolio management) for funds involves making all the investment decisions for those funds according to the fund guidelines. The team responsible for managing the fund assets works to maximize the value of the fund portfolio over time. As every fund has a specified style, asset management for the fund must reflect that. For example, with a large-cap fund, the asset management team would select specific large-cap stocks to include in the portfolio along with the relative proportion of each within it.

How it is used: Braden looked at the **asset management** team's track record for every fund he considered buying.

AUM (assets under management)

total value of securities held in a fund

What it is: a measure of the size of a mutual fund based on the current total market value of the fund's investments

How it works: AUM refers to the total market value of all securities and cash (the assets) included in a fund. Funds with higher AUMs generally trade more frequently, making it easier for investors to buy and sell fund shares. A high AUM can also indicate a fund's financial health and its ability to redeem shares without experiencing any financial difficulty. Investors considering investing in a fund can look at its AUM to get a sense of the fund's stability and resources.

How it is used: AUM was one of the factors Anita looked at when comparing similar mutual funds.

average annual returns

What it is: the amount of money earned or lost by a fund over a specific period

How it works: Average annual returns (sometimes called AAR) demonstrate a fund's past performance as an annual average, usually measured over 3, 5, or 10 years. The returns typically take into account capital gains, interest, dividends, and investment (inside the fund) share price increases. The AAR adds up the annual returns over the stated period and divides that total by the number of years being tracked. For example, if a fund had returns of 10% in year 1, 8% in year 2, and 12% in year 3, its 3-year AAR would be 10%.

How it is used: Ray wanted to invest in a fund with **average annual returns** of at least 6%.

balanced fund

fund that holds multiple asset classes

What it is: a basket of securities that includes more than one asset class

How it works: Balanced funds generally hold both stocks and bonds in a specific proportion (like 80% stocks, 20% bonds) to combine asset allocation and diversification in a single investment choice. They aim to manage risk and provide both growth and regular income. The stock portion of the fund often includes large-cap stocks and is designed to help the fund outpace inflation over time, while the bond portion provides guaranteed income and a hedge against market volatility. Balanced funds can be good choices for conservative and risk-averse investors or those nearing retirement.

How it is used: Jillian felt more comfortable with a **balanced fund** for the added security and income.

bond fund

basket of debts

What it is: a portfolio of diverse debt securities

How it works: Bond funds, which can be organized as mutual funds or exchange-traded funds, buy and sell fixed-income debt securities on behalf of investors. They may invest in Treasuries, municipal bonds, corporate bonds, or international bonds depending on the type of bond fund. Some bond funds specialize even further by limiting holdings to short-, mid-, or long-term securities. Bond funds offer investors diversity in the bond market for a relatively small investment and regular (though variable) income through interest payments. Unlike single bonds, bond funds don't have a specific maturity date.

How it is used: Garrett wanted to increase his fixed-income holdings, so he bought shares of a **bond fund**.

depreciation

wear and tear

What it is: a way to track the gradual loss of value of an asset as it's used over time

How it works: Depreciation tracks the decline in an asset's value over its useful life for tax and accounting purposes. Effectively, it's an expense that reduces taxable income without requiring any cash outlay. Depreciation is a key factor in REIT performance, as real estate (buildings, not land) depreciates over time. It's included in the calculations to determine income and taxable income. Then it gets added back into the REIT's performance metrics to show their real cash-based income.

How it is used: Depreciation lowered the REIT's taxable income but not its cash, allowing for a larger shareholder distribution.

equity REIT

real estate holding company

What it is: a company that buys, sells, and manages rental and other income-producing real estate

How it works: Equity REITs own, operate, and develop real estate assets such as apartment buildings, medical centers, and warehouses, with most of their income coming from rent. They're classified by the type of real estate they hold. Retail REITs, which hold properties like malls and grocery stores, are the largest segment among equity REITs. Other types of equity REITs include residential rental properties, assisted living facilities, office parks, warehouses, and casinos.

How it is used: Edwina bought some **equity REITs** to expand her portfolio beyond stocks and bonds.

ETF (exchange-traded fund)

basket of securities available on the secondary market

What it is: a portfolio of diverse securities bought and sold on the stock market

How it works: ETFs are securities traded over the stock exchange, where each share holds a piece of a full portfolio of other securities, offering investors instant diversification with a single investment. They're like mutual funds but are easier to buy and sell, as they trade just like stocks and can be bought and sold any time the market is open. They also offer an easier entry point for new investors, as there are no minimum investments; investors can purchase as little as a single share; and you can get started for under $100, even under $50 (including any brokerage fees or commissions).

How it is used: Chloe built a diverse beginner portfolio by buying a few shares each of different **ETFs**.

expense ratio

fees as percentage of investment

What it is: a measure of how much it will cost to have an investment in a particular fund

How it works: Expense ratios tell you how much it costs to own mutual fund or ETF shares. Higher expense ratios eat up more of your returns, so when comparing two funds, it makes sense to consider the annual costs of each. The expense ratio for a fund equals all the fund's operating expenses (such as marketing, management, and administrative fees) divided by the fund's average net assets (the average value of the fund's total holdings), and it's generally expressed as a percentage. For example, if a fund has an expense ratio of 0.20% and you have a $5,000 investment, $10 a year will come out of your holdings. A fund's expense ratio depends on the type of fund and whether it's actively or passively managed.

How it is used: Hunter compared **expense ratios** when looking at mutual funds and always chose the fund with the lowest rate.

global fund

basket of worldwide securities

What it is: an investable portfolio made up of securities from all around the world

How it works: Global funds invest in securities from multiple countries. They may focus solely on stocks, bonds, or other securities or contain an asset mix. Global funds can be set up as mutual funds or ETFs. They can focus on specific geographical areas or countries, or include a more general mix. They may also focus on the type of market: developed (countries with stable government and financial systems), emerging (fast-growing economies), or frontier (countries with the least development and stability). Investing in global funds further diversifies portfolios beyond asset allocation, adding an extra dimension for potential growth and risk balance.

How it is used: Rafael added a **global fund** to his investments to hopefully take advantage of the growth potential in emerging markets.

hybrid REIT

combination debt/asset portfolio

What it is: a basket of both property and mortgage debts designed to produce income for investors

How it works: Hybrid REITs hold a combination of physical properties and mortgages or mortgage-backed securities. Their earnings come from both rental receipts and mortgage interest. This combined style of REIT is uncommon, as most REITs focus on either real estate holdings or mortgage loans. A hybrid REIT aims to provide balanced returns to investors, delivering income regardless of whether interest rates are rising or falling. Investors who are curious about both mortgage REITs and property REITs can take advantage of this combination strategy in a single investment, rather than buying and tracking multiple securities.

How it is used: Molly and Tim wanted to own some real estate–related investments without the hassle of being landlords, so they bought shares of a **hybrid REIT**.

index fund

basket of securities that mimics a benchmark

What it is: a portfolio designed to track a published benchmark and equal the benchmark performance

How it works: Index funds, also called passive funds, are baskets of securities closely tracking a specific index like the S&P 500 (for stocks) or the Bloomberg US Aggregate Bond Index (for bonds). Investors buy shares in the index funds, giving them ownership of a piece of that entire portfolio. Their passive investment strategy helps avoid frequent active trading often used in managed funds as they attempt to outperform indexes. However, over time, index funds tend to outperform many other investments. Since the fund just mimics the makeup of its associated index, no active management is required, and that allows for lower expense ratios. Index funds can be organized as mutual funds or ETFs.

How it is used: Charlotte liked investing in **index funds** because of the simplicity and low fees.

load

sales charge

What it is: commission paid on mutual fund shares when they're traded

How it works: A load, also called a sales load, is a sales charge paid when investing in certain mutual funds (called load funds). Loads can be front end, meaning charged at the time of purchase; back end, meaning charged when the shares are sold; or level, meaning charged while the fund shares are held. Front-end and back-end loads are paid in addition to the fund's expense ratio, as they are separate fees; level loads, also called 12b-1 fees, may be included in the expense ratio.

How it is used: Jeff considered buying a mutual fund with a 0.25% front-end **load** instead of a similar no-load fund because it had performed better over the past 10 years.

managed fund

actively traded portfolio

What it is: a basket of securities where investments are adjusted as the portfolio manager sees fit to maximize investors' returns

How it works: A managed fund is a mutual fund or ETF with an actively traded portfolio. The fund manager decides which securities the fund will hold (within the fund's guidelines) and designs a portfolio that they hope will outperform the relevant market index and the markets overall. The fund manager and their team do extensive research and use their market expertise to select the investments inside the fund. These funds tend to have more taxable transactions, which can lead to higher tax bills for investors even when the fund doesn't perform well. They also tend to have higher expense ratios than index funds (unmanaged funds).

How it is used: Mitch usually avoided **managed funds** because they were more expensive and sometimes underperformed on the market.

money market fund

a portfolio of highly liquid securities

What it is: a basket of liquid, short-term securities that provides a safe place to store money temporarily

How it works: Money market funds are mutual funds that hold cash, cash equivalents, and highly rated, short-term debts to generate income for investors. These types of funds have little to no capital appreciation, meaning they do not increase in value over time. For that reason, money market funds are not generally suitable as long-term investments but instead are a place to keep funds and earn minimal income while deciding how to invest or spend the money.

Many people confuse these funds with money market *accounts*, which are bank accounts backed by federal deposit insurance. Money market funds could lose money, though they are considered extremely low-risk investments.

How it is used: Gina inherited money from her grandparents and put half of it into a **money market fund** while she decided how she wanted to invest.

mortgage REIT (mREIT)

basket of real estate loans

What it is: a portfolio composed of real estate loans and related securities that investors can buy shares in

How it works: Mortgage REITs invest in real estate debt. They can buy existing mortgages, invest in mortgage-backed securities, or act as direct mortgage lenders. They earn their income mainly through interest on the loans they hold, all of which are secured by actual real estate and sometimes also from loan servicing or loan origination fees. Like other REITs, mREITs pass 90% of their income through to shareholders as dividends. Because mREITs are directly tied to loans, their share prices and performance are highly sensitive to interest rate fluctuations, making them high-risk investments. Investors can purchase mREITs directly on the stock exchange or through mutual funds or ETFs.

How it is used: Tim decided against **mortgage REITs** for his portfolio because they were riskier than he felt comfortable with.

mutual fund

basket of securities available directly from an institution

What it is: a single investment that acts as a portfolio holding hundreds or thousands of other investments

How it works: Mutual funds pool money from many investors and use it to buy a portfolio of investments. Each investor in the mutual fund owns some of the whole portfolio and, indirectly, a share of the many different assets it includes. Mutual funds are bought and sold directly to and from the mutual fund company that issued them, even if you go through a broker for the transaction. They typically require minimum investments ranging from $1,500 to $5,000 to buy in. Mutual funds trade only once a day after the markets have closed and that day's price can be determined. Mutual fund share prices are based on the net asset value (NAV) of their investments. There are many different types of mutual funds holding practically every type of security, allowing investors to build diverse portfolios for relatively little money.

How it is used: Carina invested her 401(k) in a variety of <u>**mutual funds**</u> offered by the provider.

NAV (net asset value)

mutual fund share price

What it is: a mutual fund's worth calculated by subtracting any liabilities from the current market price of the fund's assets

How it works: The net asset value of a mutual fund equals the total market value of its assets (generally the securities it holds), subtracting any debts. This value is determined at the end of each trading day to reflect the current market price of its holdings. The total NAV gets divided by the number of outstanding fund shares to determine that day's share price. This price does not fluctuate during the day (like stock prices do) and only changes once daily after the market closes. That means the share price an investor pays today for a mutual fund won't be determined until that day's close and may not resemble yesterday's NAV. The NAV of a fund doesn't offer insights into the fund's performance because fund earnings get distributed to shareholders.

How it is used: Carter ended up buying fewer shares than expected of the mutual fund with his $2,500 investment because the **NAV** increased on the day of purchase.

niche fund

specialized investment portfolio

What it is: a basket of securities from a very narrow sector

How it works: Niche funds are funds that hold a specific narrow portfolio of investments, which could be stocks, bonds, real estate, or another asset class. These highly specialized funds aim to capitalize on small pieces of larger markets in the hopes of increased growth performance. Niches can include any specialized investment area, from video games to precious metals to Chilean holdings to space exploration. These may have less trading volume than larger, broader funds, which can impact the niche fund's liquidity (and your ability to quickly sell shares for cash).

How it is used: Marjorie bought her grandsons shares in a **niche fund** that invested stocks related to space exploration.

no-load fund

investment without a sales commission

What it is: a mutual fund that can be bought and sold without paying sales charges

How it works: No-load funds are mutual funds that don't charge commissions when the shares are bought or sold, usually directly from the fund company rather than through a broker or other sales agent. Most mutual funds are no-load funds, though there are still some that do charge commissions when their shares are traded. With no-load funds, more (often all) of the investor's money goes directly toward purchasing shares, allowing for bigger initial investments and more opportunity for compounding.

How it is used: Ryan always chose **no-load** funds for his portfolio to avoid paying sales fees.

REIT (real estate investment trust)

property-related mutual fund

What it is: a basket of income-producing properties that individual investors can buy into

How it works: REITs pool money from many investors to buy and hold income-producing real estate or real estate–related investments. While REITs can earn income from various sources, most earnings come from rental receipts. REITs must follow strict requirements to enjoy a special tax status where they pay no taxes at the company level, leaving more cash and earnings available for shareholder distributions. To qualify as a REIT, the company (among other things) must earn at least 75% of its income from real estate activities and distribute 90% of its income directly to shareholders as dividends. REITs give investors the opportunity to invest in real estate for just a few hundred dollars and the chance to own pieces of various rental properties without having to own or manage any buildings. Many REITs can be traded over the stock exchange.

How it is used: Chip always wanted to invest in real estate, and he started by buying some **REITs** for his portfolio.

stock fund

big basket of corporate shares

What it is: a portfolio of shares in many corporations that offers investors ownership of diverse equity holdings through a single investment

How it works: Stock funds are mutual funds or ETFs that invest primarily in stocks. Within this category, the fund may specialize in a particular type of stock such as blue chips, small caps, or consumer staples. Stock funds can be actively or passively managed (following an index). Stock funds allow investors to hold diversified portfolios for a relatively small investment—much less than buying individual stocks. Though most of their holdings must be stocks to qualify as a stock fund, some also hold other types of assets; you can find full information about a stock fund's holdings in its prospectus.

How it is used: Brock primarily invested in **stock funds** through his 401(k).

CHAPTER 15

Currency, Crypto, and Non-Fungible Tokens (NFTs)

The world of currency, cryptocurrency, and NFTs (non-fungible tokens) is fast, furious, and high risk. Though it might seem like these three types of assets are similar, they're actually fairly different. Investing in each type requires varied knowledge, and each is treated differently for tax purposes.

In this chapter, you'll learn the differences between currency and cryptocurrency and between crypto and NFTs. You'll discover the markets that host trading of these volatile and exciting assets, the upside potential for gains, and the downside risk of loss. This chapter explains insider terms like *airdrops*, *BTD*, *fiat currency*, and *forex* along with key principles like exchange rates, mining, and crypto wallets. You'll come away with a better understanding of how these assets can fit into your finances.

airdrop

What it is: a promotional strategy where small amounts of new crypto-currencies are sent to known crypto holders

How it works: Airdropping is a marketing method used by new players in the cryptocurrency field. It involves sending tokens to known cryptocurrency traders, directly to their wallets, hoping to generate interest in the new crypto. Airdrops may be free or in exchange for minor services like talking about the new crypto on social media. Though this is a common promotional strategy among legitimate crypto companies, it's also used by scam artists hoping to gain access to crypto wallets. Airdrops received count as taxable income in the US.

How it is used: Brad was excited to see **airdrops** in his crypto wallet when he signed up for the issuer's newsletter.

base currency

What it is: home country money used as a comparison for the value of another country's money

How it works: Base currency is a concept used on the foreign exchange (forex) market, where different countries' currencies are traded in pairs. The base currency appears first in the listed pair. For example, if you want to see the relative value of dollars (USD) to euros (EUR), the listing would be USD/EUR, where USD is the base currency and EUR is the quote currency. This listing format is useful for telling you how many units of base currency you could buy with 1 unit of quote currency; in this case, how much US dollars cost in euros.

How it is used: Julius often traded foreign currencies and preferred using US dollars as the **base currency**.

Bitcoin

What it is: a digital currency secured by blockchain technology designed for peer-to-peer usage

How it works: Bitcoin is a well-established virtual currency created to allow direct financial transactions between people and companies. This currency eliminates the need for third-party financial institutions (like banks) when sending and receiving funds. It uses blockchain technology to create bitcoins and manage their flow. Bitcoin can be mined (meaning earned by solving complex problems), bought, sold, and spent. Bitcoins trade over cryptocurrency exchanges, and investors can purchase fractional coins (a single bitcoin costs more than $90,000 as of November 2024).

How it is used: Amanda wanted to start investing in crypto so she bought as much **Bitcoin** as she could afford.

blockchain

What it is: a decentralized virtual record book that stores information in data blocks

How it works: Blockchain is a digital record book, or ledger, with no central home server. The information is decentralized and widely distributed throughout a network to record data in blocks. Each block contains specific information, including the signature of the previous block in the chain, a time stamp, and transaction details. With this setup, no block can be changed after the fact—they're irreversible. Each block is stored on many servers, and they must all match perfectly for the block to remain valid. This keeps the blockchain system secure and practically tamper-proof.

How it is used: Suzanne had a lot of confidence in **blockchain** technology; it made her feel more secure when buying Bitcoin.

BTD (buy the dip)

What it is: a trading strategy based on buying crypto (or other securities) when their price has dropped to take advantage of a potential price rebound

How it works: BTD is a strategic investment play where an investor buys assets that have (sometimes substantially) declined in value to hopefully profit when their value increases again. It's a common, age-old investing strategy—buy low, sell high—updated in today's lingo that encourages investors to purchase undervalued assets. A key factor in using this strategy successfully is recognizing a temporary price drop and acting quickly before the anticipated price rebound occurs.

How it is used: Noah was able to scoop up extra shares of crypto by using the **BTD** strategy.

cryptocurrency

What it is: a virtual form of currency that trades over decentralized exchanges rather than through traditional financial institutions like banks

How it works: Cryptocurrency (crypto) is a secure digital form of money that can be used like cash or held as an investment. Crypto transactions get recorded using blockchain technology for security and transparency. New units of cryptocurrency get mined, and existing units can be traded on crypto exchanges or used to buy goods and services. Owning cryptocurrency generally requires the use of a crypto wallet. In the US, cryptocurrency is considered to be an investment vehicle rather than cash for tax purposes, meaning most crypto transactions (except buying crypto with actual money) are taxable events. Because of its volatility, cryptocurrency can be speculative and high risk.

How it is used: Elsa bought some **cryptocurrency** because she liked the transparency of blockchain and avoiding bank fees.

crypto exchange

What it is: the online platforms that facilitate the buying, selling, and trading of digital assets

How it works: A crypto exchange is a market where you can buy and sell cryptocurrencies, like a brokerage firm for trading stocks. They offer access to generally low-fee trading over secure platforms, but it's important to research a particular exchange before using it. This space is plagued by fraud, including fraudulent or hackable exchanges. Features to look for on trustworthy exchanges include a physical address linked to the exchange, reputation and reviews, high (perhaps annoyingly so) security, trading fees, and tradable pairs (which crypto coins can be exchanged for each other). Reputable exchanges include Coinbase, Gemini, Binance, and Kraken.

How it is used: Marcus researched several **crypto exchanges** before deciding to go with one of the most secure, despite the higher fees.

crypto wallet

What it is: a key storage device that grants access to your cryptocurrency holdings in the blockchain

How it works: A crypto wallet holds the private keys that prove ownership of your cryptocurrency. These apps range in levels of complexity and security. Wallets can be physical, like thumb drives or paper, or they can be online apps. Keeping keys in a paper wallet may feel more secure, but the wallet may get lost or stolen, and accessing your crypto is more difficult (since that's held online). Hardware wallets like thumb drives offer higher security (if only connected when in use) and simplicity. Online wallets, where your keys get stored in-app, are the easiest to deal with and are secure when using a high level of encryption (two-step is preferred).

How it is used: Lewis stored his **crypto wallet** on a thumb drive that he kept in a secure lockbox.

dApp

What it is: a digital program that runs over a widely spread-out system using blockchain technology

How it works: dApps (decentralized applications) run on peer-to-peer networks and blockchain rather than on centralized servers. They're managed collectively rather than under the control of a single authority like regular apps on your phone and are used for crypto wallets and exchanges. This system prioritizes transparency, user privacy, and flexibility but may have issues with systemic upgrades, slower processing times, and security. When you use or connect to a dApp, your information goes into the blockchain and isn't collected and managed by a company.

How it is used: Fabian used his MetaMask crypto wallet to access his favorite **dApp**.

DeFi (decentralized finance)

money-related systems built on blockchain

What it is: a means of moving money online without the need for a centralized institution like a bank or brokerage

How it works: DeFi, decentralized finance, is an online financial system run on blockchain technology. This system bypasses the need for formal financial institutions to act as intermediaries to facilitate transactions. It allows people to conduct financial transactions with each other directly online, more like virtually handing someone cash rather than writing a check that needs to be processed by a bank. DeFi aims to grant access to a wider population, including people without easy access to banks, credit unions, or brokerages. It can be used for investing, lending, borrowing, and facilitating cryptocurrency transactions. However, because this technology is decentralized and fairly new, it's susceptible to scammers and hackers, which can result in theft and losses.

How it is used: Monica made a loan to someone using a **DeFi** app and earned interest without having to deal with a bank.

euro

European currency

What it is: the primary money used throughout Europe; it's one of the world's most heavily traded currencies

How it works: The euro is the main currency used by most of the nations in the European Union (EU) and a few outside it. It's one of the most widely held and heavily traded currencies in the world, second only to US dollars. In trading pairs, its symbol is EUR. Euros are worth slightly more than dollars (as of August 2024), meaning you need more than $1 to buy €1. After the euro was adopted, it gained strength by removing currency risk from trade across eurozone countries. It replaced many other currencies including the French franc, Italian lira, and German mark.

How it is used: Zoe exchanged dollars for **euros** when she went on holiday in Italy and Spain.

exchange rates

comparative currency values

What it is: the value of a country's currency when it gets traded for a different country's currency

How it works: Exchange rates are the prices involved in swapping one country's (or geographic location's) money for another's. For example, if you have dollars and want euros, the difference in their relative value would be the exchange rate. Exchange rates can be fixed or free-floating; most exchange rates are floating, meaning the amount changes constantly based on the relative strength of each country's currency. Exchange rates depend on several factors such as interest rates, unemployment levels, and other indicators of a nation's economic strength. The rates are listed in currency pairs on foreign exchanges (forex) using each country's symbol (like USD for US dollars).

How it is used: Marica hoped for favorable **exchange rates** as she set off on a European vacation.

fiat currency

government-issued money

What it is: money supported by the government rather than by something physical like gold

How it works: Fiat currency gets its value from the government that issues it rather than being backed by valuable goods like precious metals. Most paper currencies (like dollars and euros) are fiat currencies. Their value is based on the level of public confidence in their government, usually through a central bank that issued the currency. Fiat currency acts as legal tender, meaning it must be accepted as a form of payment for debts. Because it's not backed by a commodity, there's no limit to the amount of fiat currency that can be issued or printed when the government wants to increase the money supply, which has a direct impact on its value.

How it is used: Andy made his everyday purchases with dollars, a form of **fiat currency**.

foreign exchange (forex)

place to trade currencies

What it is: a market that facilitates trading one form of currency for another

How it works: The foreign exchange is a global market for exchanging different countries' currencies. It's the world's single largest market, despite being a decentralized system, and hosts trillions of dollars of trade every day. The forex allows people and businesses to buy, sell, and exchange currencies either for investment purposes or to purchase goods and services from a different country. Currencies always trade in pairs, one for another, on the foreign exchange. One common form of forex trading is a speculative strategy that seeks to capitalize on fluctuations in currency values; for example, buying euros because you think they'll increase in value compared to dollars and you'll be able to sell them later for extra dollars.

How it is used: The US dollar is the most widely traded currency on the **foreign exchange**.

fork

change in blockchain operations

What it is: a protocol change in blockchain that results in a split between the old rules and the new ones

How it works: A fork is a programming change in blockchain (like an update) that changes the way it operates. Forks can be hard or soft. A hard fork divides the blockchain into two separate blockchains, and with crypto, this creates a new cryptocurrency. Both new blockchains hold the same information (such as previous crypto transactions) up to the moment of the fork, then diverge into separate pathways. With a soft fork, the rules change but not enough to cause the formation of a second blockchain and a new cryptocurrency.

How it is used: One of Anita's crypto holdings experienced a hard **fork**, and she ended up with an equivalent amount of a different cryptocurrency.

mining

earning cryptocurrency

What it is: solving complex math programs to create new cryptocurrency coins

How it works: Mining in cryptocurrency refers to the process of adding new coins into circulation through the process of solving a highly complicated math problem on the blockchain. The first miner to solve the problem gets the coin(s). The problems involve recording and verifying blockchain transactions and creating new blocks. There's fierce competition in the mining space, and it takes sophisticated hardware and software and a lot of processing power. People mine cryptocurrency, especially Bitcoin, in the hopes they'll earn coins that appreciate in value.

How it is used: Kirsten and Larry earned some of their crypto holdings through **mining**.

NFTs (non-fungible tokens)

unique digital assets

What it is: digital assets that are not interchangeable because each one is one of a kind

How it works: NFTs are digital assets that represent ownership of something like digital artwork or videos and have been tokenized through blockchain. They're produced by content creators and artists to sell their works directly to consumers rather than through agents or galleries. Each NFT has a unique identifier that cannot be copied or divided. After their creation, encryption, and recording on blockchain (a process called minting), NFTs can be bought, sold, and traded. Common NFT categories include photography, trading cards, comic books, and music (though physical assets can also be tokenized).

How it is used: Ilaria supported several online artists and creators by buying their **NFTs**.

stablecoin

crypto with a steady price

What it is: a cryptocurrency that's tied to another currency or commodity to regulate its value

How it works: Stablecoin refers to a cryptocurrency whose value is kept relatively steady because it's pegged to an external factor, such as gold, silver, or US dollars. They often hold reserve assets to help keep tighter reins on supply and price movement. Stablecoins have less volatile price movement than other cryptocurrencies, making them more useful as a medium of exchange (for buying things, for example). They're used more like fiat currencies than for investing or trading. The top stablecoins (as of August 2024) include Tether, USD Coin, and Dai.

How it is used: Finn kept some **stablecoin** in his crypto wallet for when he needed to make purchases.

tokenize

create unique digital asset

What it is: the process creating an encrypted digital representation of ownership over blockchain

How it works: Tokenize is the process of creating a unique digital token that indicates ownership (or an ownership share) in an asset. Tokens are encrypted identification codes derived from metadata (data that gives information about other data); tokens are used to specifically identify ownership rights that can be easily tracked and traded over blockchain. Any kind of asset can be tokenized, including digital assets like videos and physical assets like real estate. Tokens can be fungible (interchangeable) or non-fungible (one of a kind).

How it is used: Gianna decided to **tokenize** her ebook and give token holders access to exclusive content.

yen

Japanese money

What it is: the primary currency of Japan

How it works: The yen (¥) is the official currency of Japan and one of the world's most widely traded currencies on the forex, coming in third right after US dollars and euros. In trading pairs, its symbol is JPY. This currency, which was adopted by Japan in the late 1800s, has been weakening in comparison with the US dollar (since 2022), largely due to increasing interest rates in the United States. A weaker yen makes it less expensive for Americans to buy goods imported from Japan and to travel in Japan.

How it is used: Petra took advantage of the weaker **yen** to book a trip to Japan when it would be more affordable.

yuan

Chinese currency

What it is: the principal unit of currency in China

How it works: The yuan (¥, or CN¥) is the main unit of currency for mainland China. The official name of the "People's Currency" is renminbi, with the yuan being the principal unit of currency, though many people use the two terms interchangeably or together (Chinese yuan renminbi). With currency trading, the Chinese yuan uses the symbol CNY. The value of the yuan was historically tightly controlled by the Chinese government, but that control has loosened somewhat as the currency began to trade internationally. The government allows some market influence on the yuan's relative value but imposes a strict trading range. The growth of the Chinese economy made the yuan one of the most used currencies in the world.

How it is used: Grace opened an account at the Bank of China in New York to hold some **yuan**.

CHAPTER 16

Retirement Planning

Retirement planning helps you to support yourself after you stop working. Plus, retirement doesn't have to mean working until your late sixties or seventies and then stopping cold turkey. It can mean designing your life in the way that best suits you, if you have the finances to fund it. This chapter goes in depth on the different kinds of tax-advantaged retirement accounts and how each can help you achieve financial goals.

In this chapter, you'll learn about the differences between Roth and traditional retirement accounts, defined benefit and defined contribution plans, and personal and workplace options. You'll find out how to avoid IRS penalties, learn more about Social Security and Medicare, and discover why pensions are great workplace benefits. This chapter provides the insights you need to create a financial plan for your retirement, whenever you want it to happen.

401(k)

What it is: an employer-sponsored retirement plan that helps employees save money for later in life

How it works: 401(k) plans are tax-advantaged retirement plans offered by private-sector employers. Employees make contributions to these retirement plans through payroll deductions. Investment choices typically include a variety of mutual funds, including target date funds and possibly some annuities. 401(k) plans can be either traditional (with pretax contributions) or Roth (with after-tax contributions) depending on the plan rules. Annual contributions are subject to IRS limits, with maximum contributions of $23,000 for 2024. Participants over 50 can make additional catch-up contributions of $7,500 per year. Employers often provide matching contributions for participating employees.

How it is used: Renata signed up for the **401(k)** at her job as soon as she was eligible because they offered a dollar-for-dollar match on up to 6% of her salary.

403(b)

What it is: a way for employees of certain government entities and non-profit organizations to save money for retirement

How it works: 403(b) plans are tax-advantaged retirement plans offered by government entities like public schools and many not-for-profit organizations. They work similarly to 401(k) plans, with the main difference being the type of employer. Employees make contributions to these retirement plans through payroll deductions. Investment choices are typically more limited in 403(b) plans than with 401(k)s but tend to offer more annuity options. Annual contributions are subject to IRS limits, with maximum contributions of $23,000 for 2024. Participants over 50 can make additional catch-up contributions of $7,500 per year. 403(b) plan participants who are not 50 but who've worked for the same employer for at least 15 years can also make special catch-up contributions of up to $15,000 over their lifetime subject to IRS annual limits.

How it is used: Donny was excited to hit his 15-year anniversary as a teacher and contribute extra money to his **403(b)** plan.

backdoor Roth

retirement account loophole

What it is: the process of converting a traditional IRA contribution to a Roth IRA by someone who wasn't allowed to make a Roth contribution

How it works: Backdoor Roth IRAs are used by high earners who couldn't otherwise contribute to Roth IRAs. This multistep process involves contributing to a traditional IRA, for which there's no income limit, and then converting that into a Roth IRA. If the traditional IRA contribution was tax-deductible, the conversion will be fully taxable; if it was made with after-tax money, the conversion may be completely nontaxable or partially taxable depending on whether any earnings have been created. The point of a backdoor Roth is to take advantage of the benefits of a Roth IRA, which include tax-free qualified withdrawals and a lack of required minimum distributions (RMDs).

How it is used: Mae earned too much to contribute to a Roth IRA, so she did a **backdoor Roth** instead.

defined benefit plan

guaranteed pension payouts

What it is: a retirement plan based on predetermined future payouts for a guaranteed steady retirement income

How it works: A defined benefit plan works like a traditional pension where the eventual payments during retirement are preset amounts. These steady, guaranteed payments make retirement budgeting easier because you know exactly how much you're going to receive periodically (usually monthly). Contributions to defined benefit plans get recalculated annually by actuaries using complex equations to support the future payouts. Companies generally get a tax deduction when they make contributions, and the payouts are taxable to the person receiving them.

How it is used: Ginger had a **defined benefit plan** through her job promising $800 a month for the rest of her life once she hit retirement age.

defined contribution plan

retirement account with steady deposits

What it is: a retirement plan where regular deposits into the plan are fixed, but eventual payouts are undetermined

How it works: Defined contribution plans are the most common retirement plans in the US. They include 401(k)s, 403(b)s, and IRAs. With these plans, you know how much money you're putting in—the defined contribution—but not how much money you'll end up being able to withdraw. The eventual withdrawals depend on a variety of factors including the amount contributed, investment choices, market performance, and timeline. The IRS determines the maximum allowable contribution for these types of plans every year, and most of them also allow an additional catch-up contribution for adults over 50.

How it is used: Mark put money into a **defined contribution plan** through his job.

early withdrawal penalty

fee for taking money prematurely

What it is: additional tax imposed by the IRS when money is taken out of a retirement plan before age 59½.

How it works: An early withdrawal penalty is an extra 10% tax charged on retirement account withdrawals taken before age 59½. This is in addition to any regular income taxes due on the withdrawal.

There are some exceptions for the early withdrawal penalty, and they vary depending on the type of account the money is being taken from; the rules for IRAs, for example, are different than the rules for 401(k)s. Some exceptions include qualified birth or adoption expenses, qualified higher education expenses, expenses due to a personal emergency, medical expenses more than 7.5% of AGI (adjusted gross income), and qualified first-time homebuyers.

How it is used: Spenser had to pay an **early withdrawal penalty** when he took money out of his 401(k) to start a business.

ESOP (employee stock ownership plan)

giving workers a stake in the company

What it is: a retirement arrangement that gives corporate shares to a company's workers

How it works: An ESOP is a type of employee benefit that gives ownership shares of the company to workers in the form of corporate stock. ESOPs are often used to give employees a financial reward for their part in the company's success and to encourage employees to stay with the company long term. The shares are usually vested, meaning that employees earn them over time, tied to their length of service. When employees leave their jobs, the company typically buys the vested shares back from them for the fair market value. Cashing out is like taking a retirement account withdrawal, so it's subject to income taxes and potentially early withdrawal penalties.

How it is used: Lucas's new employer offered an **ESOP** that fully vested shares after 4 years of employment.

full retirement age

when you can get 100% of Social Security benefits

What it is: the time when an eligible American can begin to receive 100% of their earned Social Security retirement benefits

How it works: Full retirement age (sometimes referred to as FRA) is the age at which you can get your full Social Security retirement benefits. If you begin taking benefits before then, the monthly payments will be reduced permanently; if you delay beyond that, you'll receive larger benefits. Anyone born in 1960 or later has a full retirement age of 67 but can begin taking benefits as early as age 62, receiving just 70% of benefits. The maximum Social Security retirement benefit is available to those starting at age 70, 124% of the full benefit.

How it is used: Damien wanted to wait until **full retirement age** to start collecting Social Security, but he ended up claiming benefits at age 64.

IRA (individual retirement account)
money for later

What it is: a tax-advantaged way to save money for when you stop working

How it works: IRAs give people with earned income a way to save money for retirement without having to deal with current taxes, which would slow growth. Also called traditional IRAs, these accounts allow deductible contributions (in most cases) and tax-deferred earnings.

Every year, you can contribute up to the annual maximum amount to an IRA and deduct the amount you contributed from your taxable income. That helps reduce your tax bill immediately. The contributions are invested according to your personal preferences. Any earnings on those investments, such as dividends or capital gains, don't get taxed as they're earned. Instead, all eventual withdrawals from the account get taxed at your income tax rates at the time of withdrawal.

How it is used: Grace opened an **IRA** when she got her first paycheck to start saving for retirement, planning to save the full $7,000 allowed for 2024.

matching contributions
free retirement money from employers

What it is: money an employer puts into an employee's retirement account based on the employee's contributions

How it works: Matching contributions are extra money put into your workplace retirement plan by your employer when you contribute to your personal retirement plan. These contributions don't affect the amount you're allowed to put in or increase your current taxes (unless it's a Roth-type contribution). Like the rest of the money in the retirement account, it grows tax-deferred until you begin to withdraw it. Employer-matching contributions accelerate your retirement savings. They're commonly set up to equal a percentage of the employee's contribution, such as 50% of employee contributions up to 3% of their salary. Sometimes these contributions require vesting, a delay period before the employee legally owns that money; some employers allow immediate vesting of matching contributions.

How it is used: Geri contributed 5% of her salary to her workplace 401(k) to get the full **matching contribution** from her employer.

Medicare
old age health insurance

What it is: federal health coverage for people over 65

How it works: Medicare is the federal health insurance program provided to Americans over 65 and some younger people with specific medical conditions or disabilities. Original Medicare has two parts: Part A for hospital coverage and Part B for medical coverage. Part A is free for people 65 and over who are entitled to Social Security retirement benefits, and people already receiving those benefits will be automatically enrolled in Part A once they turn 65. Part B requires premium payments for general medical coverage and must be proactively applied for; people who don't apply when first eligible will have to pay late enrollment penalties for the entire time they're covered by Part B.

How it is used: Darryl helped his mom sign up for **Medicare** a few months before she would turn 65.

pension
guaranteed retirement payments

What it is: a predictable income stream during retirement

How it works: Pensions are defined benefit retirement plans that guarantee steady, predetermined payouts to retirees. They were more common before the creation of defined contribution plans like 401(k)s, but some employers still offer them. Employers fully fund pension plans on behalf of employees. Employees don't pay tax on pension money until they receive it. The payments are based on a number of factors including how long the employee worked for the employer and their salary; they are guaranteed from the day of retirement through the full life of the employee. The payment amount is guaranteed regardless of investment performance or market conditions.

How it is used: Hope wanted a state government job so she'd have a **pension** when she retired.

post-tax

made with net pay

What it is: money that's already been subject to income taxes

How it works: Post-tax means using money that you've already paid taxes on to make retirement plan contributions. Since those contributions were already taxed, they can be withdrawn without paying additional taxes or tax penalties. Post-tax retirement accounts are known as Roth accounts and include Roth IRAs, Roth 401(k)s, and Roth 403(b) plans. These can be beneficial for people who think tax rates or their taxable income will be higher after retirement. It's also great for people who want to minimize their taxable income in retirement.

How it is used: Nancy made contributions to a **post-tax** retirement plan, a Roth IRA, so she wouldn't have to worry about taxes once she retired.

pretax

money that hasn't been taxed yet

What it is: money not included in current taxable income

How it works: Pretax means using money that has not been taxed yet to make contributions to a retirement plan. These contributions can be deducted from your paycheck before taxes are taken out or deducted from your taxable income if you don't have access to a workplace retirement plan. Pretax contributions to some self-employed retirement plans also get deducted on the tax return. Since the money in pretax (also called traditional) retirement plans has not yet been subject to income taxes, all withdrawals will be fully taxable as they're taken. Pretax retirement plans include traditional IRAs, 401(k)s, and 403(b)s.

How it is used: Francesca preferred **pretax** retirement accounts because the contributions lowered her current tax bill.

RMD (required minimum distribution)

money you must withdraw from retirement plans

What it is: the least amount you have to take out of traditional retirement accounts and pay taxes on every year

How it works: RMDs refer to the smallest withdrawal you can take from certain retirement accounts according to IRS rules. These withdrawals are mandatory for all traditional (meaning pretax) retirement accounts such as IRAs and 401(k) plans. Because the money has never been taxed before, the government requires taxable withdrawals to begin by age 73 (age 75, starting in 2033) for your own accounts (the rules are different for inherited or Roth accounts). If you fail to take a full RMD, the IRS will charge a large penalty: 25% of the amount that was supposed to be withdrawn. The rules and calculations can be confusing, so consult a professional if you aren't sure how much to withdraw to satisfy the RMD rules.

How it is used: Mara made sure to take her **RMDs** every year to avoid getting hit with IRS penalties.

Roth IRA

post-tax savings for later

What it is: a tax-favored way to save money for the future

How it works: Roth IRAs are personal retirement accounts funded with post-tax contributions that allow tax-deferred growth and tax-free withdrawals (when used properly) in retirement. Because contributions are post-tax, this money can be withdrawn at any time with no additional tax imposed. Earnings can be withdrawn tax-free after age 59½ and at least 5 years after the first contribution. Every year, eligible individuals can contribute up to the annual maximum to a Roth IRA or up to their total earned income, whichever is less, and invest that money however they choose.

Unlike other types of retirement accounts, Roth IRA contributions are subject to income limits. If you earn more than the limit, contributions may be reduced or disallowed. The income limits change annually and are based on modified adjusted gross income (MAGI).

How it is used: June chose to contribute to a **Roth IRA** because she didn't want to have to worry as much about taxes later in life.

Social Security retirement benefits

financial support for older Americans

What it is: monthly payment meant to replace a portion of earned income for people at least 62 years old

How it works: Social Security retirement benefits are monthly payments that provide income for retirees based on their lifetime earnings. As benefits are designed to replace a portion of a worker's previous income, they're normally not enough to fully cover living expenses. Eligible Americans can start collecting Social Security retirement benefits at any time between ages 62 and 70. Starting before full retirement age (usually 67) leads to permanently reduced benefits; starting at full retirement age delivers full retirement benefits; and delaying beyond that increases benefits up to the maximum allowed. Benefits are based on your top 35 years of earned income, whether at a job or self-employed, and you must have at least 10 years of earned income to qualify. In some cases, you may be eligible to collect Social Security retirement benefits based on your current or former spouse's earnings record. You can apply for and find out your projected monthly benefits at www.ssa.gov.

How it is used: Elena looked up her future expected **Social Security retirement benefits** to understand how much more she'd need to cover her postretirement expenses.

CHAPTER 17

Estate Planning

People don't like to think about dying, so they often avoid estate planning—but that's a mistake. Estate planning ensures that your possessions, money, and so on all go where you want them to after you die, and without planning, you forfeit any control. Being proactive and creating a proper estate plan can make everything easier for your friends and family in the event of your death. All you need for a usable estate plan is a set of legal documents and to add beneficiaries to your financial accounts.

In this chapter, you'll learn about what makes up an estate plan and how to make sure your wishes are known and followed. You'll find out the importance of having an advance directive, a will, and a financial roadmap for taking care of your family when you're gone. You'll understand everything from codicils to decedents to durable power of attorney. Plus, this chapter includes information about digital estates, executors, gift and estate taxes, and probate. With a solid understanding of these crucial terms, you can begin to plan for the worst and set up your family for less (financial) grief while they grieve you.

advance directive

What it is: a legal document that contains your medical care wishes in the event you're unable to communicate them

How it works: An advance directive is a legal document that tells people what medical care you do or don't want in case you can't communicate your wishes. It also appoints someone who can make healthcare decisions on your behalf. Advance directives take effect when illness or injury is so severe that a person can't make their wishes known. They typically include a living will (your care choices) and a medical power of attorney (the person who can act for you). These documents help make sure that your wishes are followed in case lifesaving measures (like CPR or being placed on a respirator) are necessary.

How it is used: Lila made sure her family knew where her **advance directive** was in the event they needed to use it.

beneficiary

asset recipient

What it is: someone who's designated to receive property or property rights from someone else, usually as an inheritance

How it works: A beneficiary is a person (or entity, like a trust) who is legally named to receive assets from someone else, usually upon their death. The assets may include life insurance proceeds, cash in bank accounts and retirement accounts, and real property. Beneficiaries can be named in wills, added to pay-on-death accounts, added to life insurance policies, and/or designated in other financial documents. In some cases, beneficiaries may need to pay tax on the assets they receive (such as with certain retirement account distributions).

How it is used: Julia was named as a **beneficiary** in her grandmother's will.

codicil

add-on rules

What it is: changes to a will without rewriting the entire legal document

How it works: A codicil is an addendum to a will, written after the will is originally signed and witnessed, that changes or further explains provisions in the will. It can be used to add or remove beneficiaries, make specific bequests (like "May gets my ruby ring"), or clarify your final wishes ("I want my ashes scattered in the Pacific Ocean"). These used to be more common when wills were handwritten and re-creating them would take a long time; they're less common now because it's just as easy to prepare a new will. To be legally accepted, a codicil must follow state law, clearly mention that it is a codicil to a specific version of a will, describe the existing provisions that will be changed, and detail the updated wishes.

How it is used: Ruby added a **codicil** to her will to make sure that if her sister and brother-in-law got divorced, Ruby's sister would be the children's guardian (rather than the couple).

decedent

dead person

What it is: a legal term used in documents for someone who has died

How it works: Decedent is the legal word for a person who died, primarily used in tax and estate planning documents. Once a person becomes a decedent, their property becomes an estate and is distributed to their named beneficiaries. Though dead, decedents do retain some legal rights, such as the right to have their final wishes carried out according to their wills or any trusts created. Decedents have legal obligations like having their last tax return filed, taxes paid, or creditors paid off; those obligations get carried out by the executor or state law if no executor is appointed.

How it is used: The **decedent** owed income taxes and state estate taxes, which came out of his estate.

digital estate

online assets

What it is: a full inventory of all online accounts and assets

How it works: A digital estate is created as part of a total estate to make sure a person's digital assets are included. Those can involve log-in information, social media accounts, email addresses, websites, and electronic records that they control. It also includes everything on a phone, tablet, computer, or flash drive, or in the cloud. Your digital estate plan details who can access these assets and how they can be accessed.

How it is used: Dmitri made sure his brother had full access to his **digital estate**, which included streaming subscriptions and gaming accounts, by adding the information to his estate plan.

durable power of attorney

substitute decision-maker

What it is: a document that gives someone the legal right to make decisions for someone else

How it works: A durable power of attorney is a legal document that gives one person the right to make decisions for another person if they can't due to illness or injury. This may include medical, financial, or legal decisions based on the details in the document. A durable power of attorney takes effect either upon document signing or when a specific event occurs. It lasts until it's revoked or the person granting the power dies.

How it is used: Laura Lee exercised the **durable power of attorney** for her father after he was diagnosed with Alzheimer's disease.

estate

everything you own

What it is: the total value of all assets someone owns minus any claims on those assets

How it works: An estate is made up of everything you own subtracting any outstanding debts, your net worth. It includes all your assets like real estate, belongings, and digital properties and all your liabilities like a mortgage and student loan debt. The value of the estate matters in cases of bankruptcy and primarily upon death. Estate planning involves deciding how you would like your assets handled/distributed when you die and preparing legal documents that spell out those wishes. In some cases, the value of an estate may be taxed upon the owner's death by the federal and state governments.

How it is used: Toby's **estate** included mainly the house he lived in and his retirement accounts.

executor

death estate manager

What it is: the person who takes care of all the bequests, debts, and expenses of an estate after someone dies

How it works: An executor is the person who carries out the intentions specified in your will, making sure your wishes are carried out. Executors can be appointed in the will or by the state and must be at least 18 years old. They are responsible for managing the assets in the estate, making sure minor children and pets are taken care of, and settling all debts associated with the estate. Their responsibilities also include things like creating an inventory of the estate, providing copies of the death certificate where needed (like to life insurance companies), preparing any estate-related tax returns, and valuing the estate for tax purposes.

How it is used: Gil was named as the **executor** in his grandmother's will, so he had to file a tax return on her behalf and took in her pet Chihuahua.

gift

something for nothing

What it is: an asset given to another person without payment in exchange

How it works: A gift is something of value given to someone else without expecting anything in return. It applies to transfers of real property (meaning real estate), personal property (physical items that are not real estate), money, securities, and any other assets to another person without receiving full value for them during the giver's lifetime. The tax code limits how much you can gift to another person annually without having to report it to the IRS. While you could give twenty different people gifts up to the limit without having to file anything, a gift to one person that even slightly exceeds the limit must be included on a gift tax return, though no tax would be due until the death of the gift giver. Gift recipients don't generally owe taxes for receiving gifts, though they may end up owing taxes if they sell it or receive income (like dividends on a gift of stock) from it.

How it is used: Angelo gave each of his children **gifts** of $10,000 every year once they turned 21.

gift and estate tax

a levy on personal assets distributed to others

What it is: a duty assessed on property transferred from one person to another either during their lifetime or upon their death

How it works: The gift and estate tax is a federal (and sometimes state) tax applied to gifts and estates over a certain value. Gifts made that exceed the annual IRS limit ($18,000 per giftee for 2024) during the gift giver's lifetime and the full value of an estate that exceeds the lifetime exclusion can be taxed. Gift and estate tax rates are graduated and range up to 40% (as of 2024) for federal tax purposes. For practical purposes, gift taxes are lumped in with estate taxes, as all are assessed at the time the estate is formed.

How it is used: Harry and Michael didn't expect the **gift and estate tax** to affect them, but they realized the value of their house, stock portfolio, and retirement accounts could put them over the limit.

guardian

person who makes decisions for someone who can't

What it is: a person named in legal documents or appointed by the court to take care of minor children or incapacitated individuals

How it works: A guardian is a person who is legally named to make financial and medical decisions for someone who can't make those decisions and may also be responsible for providing housing and care for them. The two main types of guardians are guardians of the person and guardians of the estate. Guardians of the person can make nonfinancial (like medical) decisions for the person in their charge, usually minor children or disabled adults. Guardians of the estate manage the financial affairs of an estate for the long term. Guardians can be named in someone's will or appointed by the state.

How it is used: Annabeth and George named a **guardian** for their young children in their will.

lifetime exclusion

untaxed gifts over your whole life

What it is: the amount you can transfer to other people as gifts or bequests before being taxed

How it works: The lifetime exclusion puts a cap on how much you can transfer to other people as tax-free gifts throughout your entire life. It works in connection with the annual gift tax exclusion, where any gifts that exceed that limit go toward the lifetime exclusion (also called the lifetime gift and estate tax exemption). The lifetime exclusion increased significantly in 2018 and has increased to $13.61 million (for 2024); this higher exemption will revert to pre-2018 levels starting in 2026 and drop to closer to $6 million (unless Congress steps in). Anything over the lifetime exclusion, which includes taxable gifts made during life and the total estate value on death, will be subject to gift and estate taxes.

How it is used: Henry took advantage of the **lifetime exclusion** to make sure his kids wouldn't have to deal with gift and estate taxes when he died.

POD (pay on death) designation

automatic asset transfer

What it is: a direct transfer of assets to a beneficiary after the owner dies

How it works: A POD designation, also called a Totten trust, adds a named beneficiary to a financial account so that it will transfer automatically to the beneficiary upon the owner's death. PODs can be added to most bank accounts, including savings, checking, and CDs (certificates of deposit). This strategy avoids probate, so the beneficiary has quicker, easier access to assets.

The POD designation also supersedes a will, meaning that if an account is left to someone in a will and someone else is named as the POD beneficiary, the POD beneficiary will prevail. A similar arrangement called TOD (transfer on death) is available for investment accounts.

How it is used: Marcy named her granddaughter in the **POD designation** on all her bank accounts.

probate

asset distribution after someone dies

What it is: the legal process of distributing a decedent's assets according to their will or state law

How it works: Probate is a legal process of distributing a deceased person's assets. When there's a will, the probate process validates the will and oversees its administration. Without a will, a situation called intestate, the state determines how the decedent's assets will be distributed and debts settled. This process can take weeks or months, leaving beneficiaries waiting to receive their bequests. Probate laws vary by state and often depend on factors such as estate size, marital status of the decedent, outstanding debts, and whether any real estate or vehicles are involved. Probating with a will is generally faster and less expensive than going through the process with no will.

How it is used: Manuel and Rosa created an estate plan so that many of their assets could avoid going through **probate**.

trust

legal vessel for asset management

What it is: a legal agreement that creates a special account to hold and manage assets on behalf of beneficiaries

How it works: A trust is a legal document that creates an arrangement to manage assets for named beneficiaries. Trusts are often used in estate planning; they can be used while you're alive (a living trust) or created upon your death (a testamentary trust). They're set up and carried out in accordance with your wishes and allow you to transfer your assets during or after your lifetime without the need for probate court. Trust documents (unlike wills) are private documents and may help protect assets against taxation, creditors, and lawsuits. A trust can be revocable, meaning you can change or cancel it at any time, or irrevocable, meaning it is permanent and unmodifiable.

How it is used: Zoe set up a **trust** with herself and her partner as beneficiaries as part of her estate plan.

will

final wishes

What it is: a legal document that spells out exactly how you want your property distributed upon your death

How it works: A will, also called a last will and testament, is a public legal document where you determine how you want your assets to be distributed and who you want to look after any minor children when you die. If you die without a will (called intestate), the courts will decide who will care for your children and how your assets will be parceled out, generally according to the laws of your home state. Having a will makes your final wishes clear and makes it easier for your heirs to access your property. You don't need a lawyer to write a will, but for it to be valid and work in the desired fashion, it must be worded correctly according to state law. Most states require that wills be signed and witnessed to be considered valid. Along with written wills (the most common form), some states accept holographic wills (signed but not witnessed).

How it is used: Tom appointed his sister as the guardian of his kids in his **will** and left all his assets in trust for them.

Index

Assistance programs: homeownership vouchers, 123–24; Lifeline for phone/Internet, 39; LIHEAP (home energy assistance), 39–40; Medicaid, 72; Section 8 (housing), 40–41; SNAP (food support), 41; SSDI, 28; SSI, 28–29; TANF (temporary assistance), 41–42; WAP (weatherization assistance), 43; WIC (food support for moms), 44

Auto loans (*See also* Debt, dealing with): about, 116; ACV (actual cash value), 114; base price and, 116; secured loans and, 113, 125; trade-ins and, 126; underwriting, 126

Banking and financial services, 7–19 (*See also* Financial planning; Income and net worth; Investing; Savings); ACH (Automated Clearing House), 8; assets explained, 22; ATM fees, 8; available balance, 9; bank services fees, 9–10; brokers and brokerage accounts, 10–11; cash equivalents, 11; checking accounts, 11; commissions and, 12; credit unions, 13; debit cards and, 13–14; debit transactions, 14; depositors and, 14–15; direct deposit, 22; equity explained, 23; financial advisors, 15; gross pay, 23–24; joint accounts, 16; liabilities and, 24; liquidity and, 24–25; NSF (non-sufficient funds), 16–17; overdrafts, 17; transfers (of money), 17–18; withdrawals, 18–19

Bitcoin, 176. *See also* Currency, crypto, and NFTS

Bonds. *See* Stocks and bonds

Borrowing money. *See* Auto loans; Credit cards; Loans and borrowing money; Mortgages and home loans; Personal loans; Student loans

Budgeting (*See also* Financial planning): automatic payments and, 34; budgets explained, 34–35; envelope method (cash stuffing), 36; 50/30/20 splits, 33; overview of financial planning and, 32; supplementary assistance programs (*See* Assistance programs); zero-balance budget, 44

Credit (*See also* Credit cards; Loans and borrowing money): about: borrowing money and, 78; credit checks, 82; FICO score, 84–85; limits, 82–83; report, 83; score, 83–84; transactions, 12–13; utilization, 90

Credit agency, 81

Credit cards, 91–99; about: overview of, 91; annual fee, 92; APR (annual percentage rate), 92; authorized users, 93; average daily balance, 93; balance transfers, 94; cash advances, 94–95; credit limits, 95; debit cards and, 13–14; grace periods, 95–96; late payment fees, 96; minimum monthly payment, 96–97; over-limit fee, 97; penalty APR, 97–98; rewards, 98; secured, 98; Truth in Lending Act and, 111; variable interest rate, 99; zero-balance cards, 99

Crypto. *See* Currency, crypto, and NFTS

Currency, crypto, and NFTS, 174–85; about: overview of, 174; airdrop strategy, 175; base currency, 175;

Bitcoin, 176; blockchain, 176; BTD (buy the dip), 177; cryptocurrency explained, 177; crypto exchange, 178; crypto wallet, 179; dApp, 179; DeFi (decentralized finance), 179; digital estates and, 199; euro currency, 180; exchange rates, 180; fiat currency, 181; foreign exchange (forex), 181; fork (blockchain change), 182; mining (earning crypto), 182; NFTs (non-fungible tokens), 183; stablecoins, 183; tokenize explained, 184; yen (Japanese currency), 184; yuan (Chinese currency), 184–85

Debt, dealing with, 127–38 (See also Auto loans; Credit; Credit cards; Loans and borrowing money; Mortgages and home loans); about: overview of, 127; arrears, 128; avalanche method (prioritizing high-rate payments), 129; bankruptcies and, 129–30; charge-offs, 131; collections, 131; credit counseling, 132; debt consolidation, 132–33; debt settlement, 133; default (nonpayment), 133–34; deferments, 134; delinquency, 134–35; Fair Debt Collection Practices Act (FDCPA), 135; financial fix-up bankruptcy, 130; forbearance, 135–36; garnishment and, 136; liquidation bankruptcy, 130; payment plans, 136–37; payoff amount, 137; phantom debt, 137–38; snowball method, 138; validation notice, 138

Estate planning, 196–204; about: overview of, 196; advance directives, 197; beneficiaries, 197; codicil (add-on rules), 198; decedents and, 198; digital estates and, 199; durable power of attorney and, 199; estate defined, 199–200; executors and, 200; gifts, gift and estate tax and, 200–201; guardians and, 201–2; lifetime exclusions and, 202; POD (pay on death) designation, 202–3; probate and, 203; trusts and, 203–4; wills and, 204

Exchange-traded funds (ETFs). See Mutual funds, ETFs, and REITs
Expenses (See also Budgeting; Financial planning; Taxes): essential, 36–37; fixed, 38; tax deductions and, 54; variable, 42–43

Financial planning (See also Budgeting; Investing; Mutual funds, ETFs, and REITs; Savings): CFPs (certified financial planners) for, 35; diversification and, 35–36; fiduciaries and, 37; financial advisors and, 15; financial goals and, 37–38; inflation and, 38–39; time value of money and, 42
Funds. See Mutual funds, ETFs, and REITs

Income and net worth, 20–31 (See also Financial planning; Investing; Savings; Taxes); about: overview of, 20–31; debt-to-income ratio, 84 (See also Credit; Loans and borrowing money); earned income, 22–23, 47–48; equity explained, 23; garnishment and, 136 (See also Debt, dealing with); gross pay, 23–24, 25; net pay, 25; net worth explained, 25–26; passive income, 26; salary, 27; self-employment income, 27–28; SSDI, 28; SSI, 28–29; supplementary assistance programs (See Assistance programs); unemployment benefits and, 29; wages, 30–31
Insurance, 64–77; about, 64; actual cash value and, 65; annuity, 65–66; auto, 66; brokers, 70; claimants, 66–67; collision, 67; comprehensive, 67; deductibles, 68; disability, 28, 71–72, 75–76; good driver discounts, 68; health, 69; homeowners, 69–70; life, 70–71, 76, 77; long-term care, 71; long-term disability, 71–72; Medicaid, 72; Medicare, 192; PMI (private mortgage insurance), 124; policies, 72–73; premiums, 73; premium tax credits (PTC), 73–74; renters, 74; replacement cost and, 74; riders (endorsements), 75;

short-term disability, 75–76; term life, 76; umbrella, 76; variable universal life (VUL), 77; whole life, 77

Interest (earned) (*See also* Savings): about (defined), 61; compound, 59; high-yield accounts (HYSA) and, 60–61; money market/savings accounts earning, 60–62, 63; simple, 62–63

Interest (expense) (*See also* Debt, dealing with): accrued interest, 128; credit card, 92, 99

Investing, 139–49 (*See also* Estate planning; Mutual funds, ETFs, and REITs; Stocks and bonds): about: overview of, 139; accredited investors, 140; asset allocation, 33–34; asset classes, 140; asset management, 163; benchmarks, 141; capital gains (or losses), 141–42; commodities and, 142; compounding earnings, 142–43; cost basis, 143; diversification and, 35–36; the Dow (DJIA) and, 143–44; ESG (environmental, social, and governance) investing, 144; indexes explained, 144–45; Nasdaq and, 145; NYSE (New York Stock Exchange) and, 145–46; portfolios, 146; returns (earnings), 146–47; risk/reward ratio, 147; risk tolerance, 147–48; S&P 500 (Standard & Poor's 500), 148; trading and, 149

Loans and borrowing money (*See also* Auto loans; Credit cards; Mortgages and home loans; Personal loans; Student loans): about: credit and, 78 (*See also* Credit); amortization, 79; balloon payments, 79; bridge loans, 80; cosigners, 80–81; credit builder loans, 81–82; debt-to-income ratio, 84; liens and, 85; loan balance, 86; loans explained, 85–86; negative amortization, 86–87; non-revolving debt, 87; preapproved, 87–88; predatory lending and, 108; promissory notes (IOUs), 88; quotes on, 88–89; refinancing, 89; revolving

debt, 89–90; utilization (credit utilization ratio), 90

Money market. *See* Interest (expense); Mutual funds, ETFs, and REITs

Mortgages and home loans (*See also* Debt, dealing with): about, 124; adjustable rate mortgages (ARMs), 115; appraisals and, 115; biweekly payments, 117; buydowns, 117–18; closing costs, 118; deeds and, 118–19; down payments, 119; earnest money, 119–20; escrow and, 120; FHA (Federal Housing Administration) and, 120–21; 5/1 RM (adjustable-rate mortgage), 114; fixed rate loans, 121–22; FTHB (first-time homebuyers) programs, 121; HELOC (home equity line of credit), 122; HOAs (homeowners associations) and, 122–23; home equity loans, 123; homeownership vouchers, 123–24; PMI (private mortgage insurance), 124; prepayment penalties, 125; secured loans and, 113, 125; underwriting, 126

Mutual funds, ETFs, and REITs, 162–73; about: overview of, 162; asset management, 163; assets under management (AUM), 163; average annual returns, 164; balanced funds, 164; bond funds, 164–65; depreciation and, 165; equity REITs, 165–66; ETFs (exchange-traded funds), 166; expense ratio, 166–67; global funds, 167; hybrid REITs, 167–68; index funds, 168; loads (sales charges), 168–69; managed funds, 169; money market funds, 169–70; mortgage REITs (mREITs), 170; mutual funds, 170–71; NAV (net asset value), 171; niche funds, 171–72; no-load funds, 172; REITs (real estate investment trusts), 172–73; stock funds, 173

Personal finance, this book and, 5–6

Personal loans (*See also* Student loans): about, 100, 107; application fee, 101; origination fee, 105; payday loans, 106;

predatory lending and, 108; repayment term, 109; Truth in Lending Act and, 111; unsecured loans, 111; usury laws and, 112

Real estate investment trusts (REITs). *See* Mutual funds, ETFs, and REITs

Retirement planning, 186–95 (*See also* Estate planning); about: overview of, 186; backdoor Roth IRAs, 188; defined benefit plans, 188–89; defined contribution plans, 189; early withdrawal penalties, 189–90; ESOPs (employee stock ownership plans), 190; 401(k) plans, 187; 403(k) plans, 187–88; full retirement age, 190–91; IRAs (individual retirement accounts), 191; matching contributions, 191–92; Medicare and, 192; pensions, 192–93; post-tax explained, 193; pretax explained, 193; RMDs (required minimum distributions), 194; Roth IRAs, 194–95; Social Security retirement benefits, 195

Savings, 56–63 (*See also* Budgeting; Financial planning; Interest (earned); Investing; Mutual funds, ETFs, and REITs); APY (annual percentage yield), 57–58; balance, 58; CDs (certificates of deposit), 58; deposits, 59–60; emergency fund, 60; 529 plans, 57; high-yield accounts (HYSA), 60–61; money market accounts, 61; online accounts, 62; PYF (pay yourself first) rule, 40; targeted accounts, 63; traditional accounts, 63

Stock funds, 173

Stocks and bonds, 150–61 (*See also* Investing); about: overview of, 150; blue chip stocks, 151; bond discount, 151; bond premiums, 152; bonds explained, 141; common stock, 152; corporate bonds, 152–53; dividends, 153; I-bonds (inflation protection), 153–54; junk bonds, 154; large cap stocks, 154; market capitalization, 155; micro cap, 155; mid cap, 156; municipal bonds, 156; par value, 157; preferred stock, 157; series EE bonds, 158; shares, 158; small cap, 159; stocks explained, 148–49; treasury bills, 159; treasury bonds, 160; treasury notes, 160; yields, 160–61

Student loans (*See also* Debt, dealing with): about, 100, 110–11; direct subsidized loan, 101; direct unsubsidized loan, 102; FAFSA (Free Application for Federal Student Aid), 102; forbearance, 135–36; graduated repayment plan, 103; IBR (income-based repayment) plan, 103–4; ICR (income-contingent repayment) plan, 104; loan servicers, 104–5; NSLDS (National Direct Student Loan Data System), 105; origination fee, 105; PAYE (Pay As You Earn) plan, 106; PLUS loans, 107; PSLF (public service loan forgiveness) program, 108–9; repayment term, 109; Sallie Mae, 109–10; SAVE (Saving on a Valuable Education) plan, 110; Truth in Lending Act and, 111

Taxes, 45–55 (*See also* Estate planning); above-the-line deduction, 46; AGI (adjusted gross income), 46–47; capital gains tax, 47; deductions, 49, 54; defined, 53; earned income, 47–48; filing status, 48; income tax, 49; itemized deductions, 49; MAGI (modified adjusted gross income), 50; marginal rate, 50; property tax, 51; sales tax, 51; self-employment taxes, 52; standard deductions, 52; taxable income, 54–55; tax brackets, 53; tax credits, 54; Form 1040, 48; 1099 form, 21; W-2 forms, 29–30; W-4 forms, 30